S0-AQM-258

ILE: A First Look

**George
Farr**

**Shailan
Topiwala**

foreword by
Jon Paris & Susan Gantner

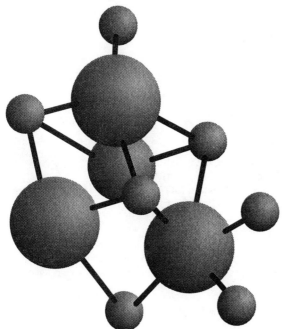

ILE
A First Look

George Farr & Shailan Topiwala

foreword by
Jon Paris & Susan Gantner

ILE: A First Look by George Farr & Shailan Topiwala

Published by:
Computer Applications Specialists, Inc.
Education Group
4715 Sellman Rd., Beltsville, MD 20705
President: Carson Soule
Publisher: Merrikay B. Lee
Senior Editor: Karen Forster
Graphic Design: Scott Lee

Editorial Review Board:
Carson Soule, CDP, CCP, CSP, President, CAS, Beltsville, MD
Mike Dawson, CDP, Consulting by Nerds, Flagstaff, AZ
Virgil Green, SynapTech Consulting, St. Louis, MO
Trevor Perry, President, Prolific Software, Arlington, TX
Rick Turner, Rick Turner Assoc., Rochester, MN
Jonathan Yergin, CDP, Gainesville, GA

All Rights Reserved. No part of this book may be reproduced in any manner, in whole or in part, in English or in other languages, in hard copy or in electronic media without written permission from the publisher except for brief quotations in books, magazine articles, or critical reviews.

Copyright © 1994 by Computer Applications Specialists, Inc.
Beltsville, Maryland
Printed in the United States of America
First Printing: March, 1994

This work was prepared by the authors and the technical and editorial staff of Computer Applications Specialists, Inc. Every effort has been made to ensure that the techniques and procedures included in this book are accurate. While each item has been reviewed by the authors and CAS, Inc., there is no guarantee implied or expressed that the same or similar results will be obtained elsewhere. Readers attempting to adapt these techniques to their own environments do so at their own risk. At the time of printing this text, ILE RPG is a statement of direction from IBM. The screens and examples in this book are based on information provided by IBM in public presentations, magazine articles and other public forums and may therefore not match the final product exactly.

This book is not sponsored in any part or in any manner by the IBM Corporation. IBM does not endorse or represent the accuracy or appropriateness of any information contained herein. In addition, this book is not intended to replace IBM product documentation or personnel in determining the specifications or capabilities of the included products. The reader is responsible for choice of all configurations and applications of computer hardware and software. The reader should discuss his choice of alternatives with the appropriate IBM representative.

TRADEMARKS: All company and product names are registered trademarks or trademarks of their respective owners.

ISBN 1-884322-22-0

For my darling Carolyn,
for her faith, patience,
and most of all,
her wisdom

— *Shailan*

To my father
Neiman I. Farr
and my pillars of strength,
my wife Diana and
my children Angelica and Michael

— *George*

ACKNOWLEDGMENTS

We would like to take this opportunity to thank several people for their valuable contributions to the text.

From IBM Rochester, we would like to thank the following people for helping to ensure the technical accuracy of the text.

Terry Ackman
Susan Gantner
Frank Benson
Joel Eikenhorst
Jing Wang

From IBM Toronto, thanks to the following people for taking the time to review our work.

Jon Paris
Mark Stankevicius
Sal Visca

Also, we would like to express our gratitude to Karen Forster and Merrikay Lee of CAS Publishing who have been a absolute joy to work with. We have learned a great deal from them both and look forward to working together on future projects.

Last, we would like to express our heartfelt appreciation to Carolyn Topiwala and Diana Farr. They have given their time in helping to proof the text, but more important, without their encouragement, advice, and support, this work would have not been possible.

— *George and Shailan*

Table of Contents

Chapter 4: Binding   35

Chapter 5: Service Programs   43

Chapter 6: Binding Directories   55

Chapter 10: Source-Level Debugging   109

Chapter 11: Frequently Asked Questions   125

Chapter 12: What's Next... 153

Appendix A: CL Commands 155

Appendix B: APIs 157

Glossary 163

Index 177

Foreword

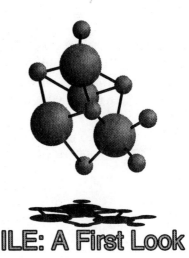

ILE: A First Look

Of all the subjects George and Shailan could have chosen to write about, the Integrated Language Environment (ILE) is probably the toughest. We should know — we've devoted a considerable amount of time and energy to trying to teach this topic over the past year or so. We've worked on everything from ILE manuals, to training videos, field support materials, user group presentations, magazine articles . . . Well, you get the picture.

The one thing we learned very quickly was that this is not an easy subject to teach. Don't misunderstand. ILE is not that complicated. (After all, how complicated can something based on zeros and ones get?) The complexity arises mainly in two areas: First, the number of completely new (for an AS/400 programmer) principles that need to be absorbed; and second, the fact that so many of the topics involved are somewhat circular in nature. That is, to understand topic C you need some understanding of topic B. To understand B you need to understand A, but to understand A —guess what— you need to understand C!

So, when we were asked to write the foreword to this book, we were truly delighted. (After all, it meant that CAS wouldn't be chasing us to write it!) Now that we've had a chance to read the book, we find ourselves even happier. George and Shailan have done a remarkable job of making sense out of a very difficult and important subject.

"Important?" Yes. ILE is probably the most significant change ever made to the AS/400. In fact, we'd probably go so far as to say that ILE represents a bigger change than the transition from the System/38.

ILE is the underpinning for the future of the AS/400. As we move into the new world of object oriented programming, application frameworks, etc., the principles embodied in ILE will assume greater and greater significance to you as an AS/400 programmer.

So, come on in! The water's fine. Let George and Shailan act as your swimming instructors as you "dive" into ILE. Enjoy.

Jon Paris   Susan Gantner
AS/400 Languages   Marketing Support
Strategy & Planning   AS/400 Competency Center
IBM Toronto Laboratory   IBM Rochester Laboratory

Introduction

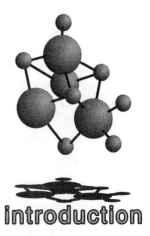

In the past, efficiency has been a great issue when AS/400 programmers have considered modular applications that might include components written in various HLLs (high-level languages). Because interest in modular, interlanguage programming methodologies has been rapidly increasing, IBM has addressed this issue by developing ILE (Integrated Language Environment). If you create call-intensive or mixed-language applications you will find that ILE makes your work easier and your applications more efficient.

As an AS/400 professional, you've probably heard about ILE but haven't found a lot of information about what it really is and does or how it relates to you. That's the reason for this first look at ILE: to give you a clear and concise explanation of not only the new functionality, but also the concepts and terminology ILE introduces. Although this first look is not intended as an in-depth guide to programming in ILE, we've added coding examples of ILE RPG and other ILE languages to clarify the explanations of ILE.

Of course, your first question is probably, "What is ILE?" Well, unlike RPG, C, or COBOL, ILE is *not* a language. Rather it is the underlying environment that enables all the newly introduced ILE languages to work together. In fact, ILE is not really an environment, either, in the sense of the S/36 environment, for example. Unlike such environments, ILE will let you mix all your old applications written in, say RPG/400, with all new applications written in ILE RPG. You can think of ILE as providing an additional operating-system function that gives you improved application performance and code reusability in mixed-language and call-intensive applications.

As we've said, IBM introduced ILE with OS/400 V2R3 (Version 2 Release 3) to improve performance of single- or multilanguage applications that are call intensive, to promote modular programming and mixed-language applications, and to let you take advantage of the particular strengths of each HLL. For example, RPG is a good choice for report formatting and printing, and C is suited to compute-intensive applications; in ILE, you can write a particular application's reports in RPG and perform the same application's computations using C. In addition, ILE improves performance by providing new types of program calls.

To create interlanguage ILE applications, you write code in any ILE-supported HLL (ILE RPG/400, ILE COBOL, ILE CL, or ILE C/400). That code is compiled into an intermediate language by means of a new command, CRTxxxMOD (where xxx stands for a particular ILE language, such as RPG). Then the AS/400 Common Use Back-End compiles the code produced by the compilers and calls the binder. The binder and optimizing translator create the *MODULE object. Then, when you execute the new CRTPGM command, the *PGM object is created. Because all ILE languages are compiled into the same intermediate language, you can easily use ILE RPG, C, and COBOL modules within one application. For example, Figure I-1 illustrates how you can mix ILE RPG and ILE C in one application.

In this example, the payroll application, which is written in ILE RPG, calls the numeric function,

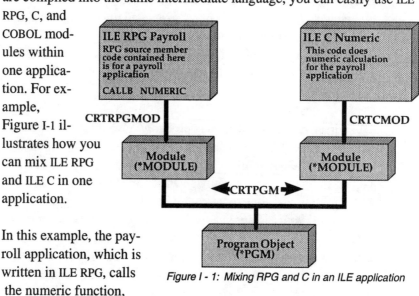

Figure I - 1: Mixing RPG and C in an ILE application

which is written in ILE/C, to do some arithmetic calculation. Note that a new RPG operation code, CALLB, tells the compiler to use the ILE method of calling the C procedure. (We will explain all this in the course of this book.)

As this example illustrates, you first compile the ILE RPG code using the CRTRPGMOD (Create RPG Module) command to produce the intermediate result (i.e., the first program module). Second, you execute the CRTCMOD (Create C Module) command to produce the corresponding C module. Finally, you execute the CRTPGM command to glue both these pieces of the application together to produce an executable program (of object type *PGM) that contains both modules.

Naturally, this quick overview is pretty simplistic, so you need to know more about ILE: what it replaces and improves on and what its components and new features are. To explain all that, we'll start with a chapter on ILE's history. That chapter discusses ILE's predecessors and explains what ILE provides that they didn't. Then, to introduce ILE programming, we have a chapter on how to create an ILE program. This chapter brings up the concepts of modules, binding, service programs, and binding directories, and each of these is then the topic of a succeeding chapter. Next, we explain how ILE program activation functions, how it differs from that in ILE's predecessor environments, and how it works with those environments. The following chapter discusses new APIs, and the one after that outlines the ILE exception-handling model and its benefits. If you're looking for a little refreshment at this point, the last two chapters should be just what you need. You'll get a chance to go step-by-step through debugging in the new environment, and finally, you'll get to see the answers to the most frequently asked questions about ILE. To sum it all up, the concluding chapter addresses likely future developments in programming on the AS/400. An appendix of ILE-related CL commands, an appendix of all the new ILE APIs, and a glossary close the book.

ILE is part of the ongoing evolution of AS/400 programming languages. IBM has developed ILE in response to user needs and as a bridge to future developments, such as visual programing with GUIs (graphical user inter-faces) and use of OOP (object-oriented programming). In preparation for this book's discussion of the details of ILE, to understand its significance, and to learn what problems it solves, let's review the evolution that has resulted in ILE.

History

ILE's predecessors were the AS/400's OPM (Original Program Model) and EPM (Extended Program Model). When IBM developed OPM, RPG and COBOL were by far the most prevalent compilers AS/400 programmers used, so OPM was designed to be most considerate of applications in those languages. (In 1988, when the AS/400 was announced, RPG, COBOL, PL/I, and BASIC were the only HLLs OS/400 supported.)

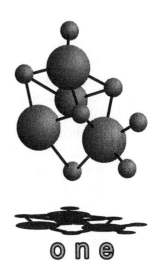

OPM treats each program as an independent object capable of accessing other program objects via an *external* call. An external (or *dynamic*) call implies that the calling program object (*PGM object) does not contain the program object the call will execute. In RPG/400, for example, when you use the CALL operation code, it will execute a different program (*PGM object) from the one that contains the CALL, as shown in Figure 1-1.

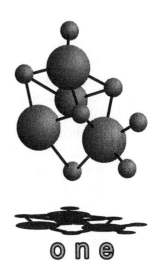

Figure 1 - 1: Dynamic call in
RPG/400 OPM

As the figure shows, under OPM, you code your source and then execute the CRTRPGPGM (Create RPG Program) command to create your executable object, your *PGM. At the time you create the calling program, the program you want to call, PGM1 in Figure 1-1, does not have to exist on the system. However, it must exist at runtime (i.e., at the time you execute the program) because the runtime environment will search the library list to resolve this called object (i.e., locate it, perform any security validation, etc.). Because resolution occurs at runtime, we refer to such calls as dynamic calls. Once the object is resolved, the system performs required initialization and authority checks and finally executes the program (*PGM object) being called.

The two main advantages of the OPM environment are 1) that you compile your programs into executable objects by performing only one step and 2) that you can easily replace a program at both the application service and development levels if you need to update or change a program. For example, in OPM if you have to replace PGM1, you can just delete the *PGM object and re-create it by recompiling. As you saw in Figure 1-1, in the OPM environment, you only have to execute a create command (such as CRTRPGPGM or CRTCBLPGM) to get your executable object. This is what we refer to as a one-step program creation. In contrast, as this book will explain in detail, in ILE, you have to recompile the individual program modules that you want to be a part of the *PGM object and then bind these modules together as one executable program.

Although effective, OPM's one-step program creation process also has its disadvantages, mainly in terms of performance. For call-intensive applications, OPM execution performance is poor. In addition, dynamic calls require many processor clock cycles to perform the five steps (resolution, authority verification, system initialization, program initialization, and program execution) necessary to resolve the program.

1. *Resolution*: The library list is searched to find the referenced program and return its handle (address) to the calling program so that the system can locate and call the referenced program.

2. *Authority verification*: The system verifies that the calling program has the appropriate authority level to call this object.

3. *System initialization*: Because the called program is external code, the system sets up a new call frame for the program's execution.

4. *Program initialization*: The system initializes the program.

5. *Program execution*: The system executes the program.

Because of these performance problems, most OPM programmers avoid call-intensive designs and develop large, multifunction programs that require a lot of maintenance. And, such programs are difficult to maintain. In addition, source compilation and program startup are time consuming under OPM.

In spite of these shortcomings, OPM languages remained the mainstay of most AS/400 programmers. However, as the AS/400 system grew in size and functionality, programmers began demanding access to modern programming methodologies and the procedural languages that facilitated them.

OPM did not support procedural languages, such as C, FORTRAN, and Pascal. These languages differ from OPM languages in that procedural languages have scoped fields, automatic fields, external fields, multiple entry points, and frequently called functions or procedures. Because OPM did not support these features, IBM developers had to build a new environment to accommodate procedural languages. This new environment was EPM.

Extended Program Model (EPM)

Procedural languages gained popularity because commercial application design methodology was moving towards the top-down design method, which requires breaking down an application into discrete, reusable modules. In contrast to languages like RPG and COBOL, procedural languages have certain characteristics that suit them to top-down methodology but not to the OPM environment. The development of EPM was necessary to support the following characteristics of procedural languages.

- Procedural languages support functions or procedures that let you easily break down the solution.

- Procedural languages support parameter passing to those functions or procedures, so that you can make inputs and outputs clear.

- Procedural languages provide data scoping. This point is related to the declaration and definition of variables at the head of any program block to make clear to the reader of that program which variables the following code can affect.

- Procedural languages provide an efficient means of calling other programs. One key observation here is that procedural languages encourage call-intensive designs, something OPM handles poorly. Another relevant point is that procedural languages support programs with multiple entry points, which let you begin execution from more than one point in a program, depending on the function desired. RPG and COBOL permit only one point at which execution can begin within a given program. Programs in languages such as C, on the other hand, may consist entirely of functions, without any mainline as such, and each function may be an entry point for that program module. This flexibility lets you prevent certain groups of code, based on function, from using that function, without regard for how performance will be affected.

- Procedural languages permit data sharing across program boundaries. This refers to the ability to define data in one program and use it in another. In most procedural languages, such a feature would be termed "externalization of variables."

Unfortunately, RPG and COBOL were not suited to this method. Take, for example, OPM RPG. Its syntax does not encourage modular programming. RPG supports subroutines, but they are implemented as branch points within the same program, and you may not pass parameters to those subroutines. Another obstacle to modular programming is that RPG requires you to formally declare program data at the top of the program, so it is difficult to make clear which data the following program block can or cannot affect. And, closely related to this problem is the fact that RPG does not permit data scoping. Finally, calls to other programs (modules) imply a dynamic call.

When IBM introduced procedural languages to the AS/400, IBM developers had to address OPM's lack of facilities to handle features such as multiple entry points, external data sharing, scoping and nested scoping, and call intensiveness. The solution was to extend OPM and create EPM. As Figure 1-2 shows, EPM was not an integrated part of the operating system, but a layer over OPM. All EPM language and environment features existed as a second layer over the OPM environment, and EPM used OPM features such as messaging, exception handling, and initialization. As a result, EPM was not an ideal solution. Mixed OPM and EPM applications were far from seamless and usually didn't perform as expected. EPM did not fill all of AS/400 developers' requirements for mixed-language and call-intensive application support. This lack of full support for procedural languages led to ideas of a new environment, ILE.

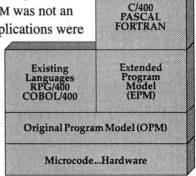

Figure 1 - 2: OPM and EPM application

OPM, EPM, and ILE

Conventional wisdom in the midrange environment says that typical applications are never rewritten. Rather, over the course of many releases of the operating system, programmers replace certain program components in an effort to harness the new function or languages that come with each release. Such ever-evolving applications, for obvious reasons, are termed *legacy* applications. Legacy code carries its function over many releases of both the operating system and hardware. Thus, when IBM considered the need for a new environment to facilitate multilanguage applications on the AS/400, developers were aware of the need to keep legacy applications viable.

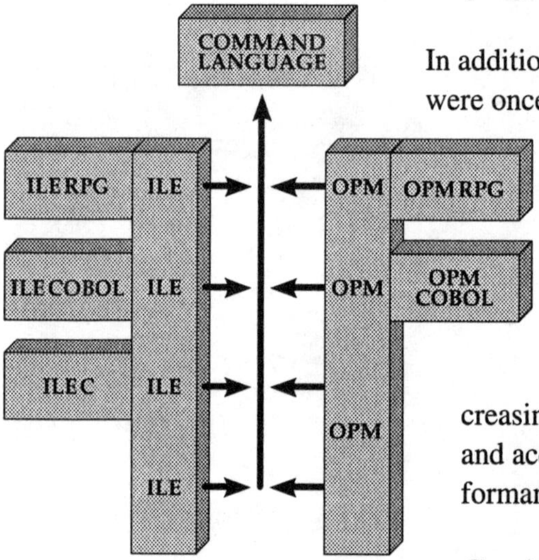

In addition, many AS/400 applications that were once strictly RPG now integrate components written in C. The need for C support has been growing, especially because of the need for portability and compatibility across various platforms. So a solution to the problem of multilanguage applications also had to answer increasing demand for C-language support and account for compile and execution performance issues.

Figure 1 - 3: ILE in conjunction with OPM

Consideration of legacy code, the need for better system performance, and support for both OPM and EPM languages led to ILE, the solution Figure 1-3 illustrates. Within the OPM execution model, a program object in any EPM or OPM language has call access to program objects in any other EPM or OPM language. In the same way, within the ILE execution model, the ILE languages have access to each other. In addition, OPM, EPM, and ILE can interact directly, as well as through CL, which serves as an interface to all three language categories.

ILE supports both OPM and EPM runtime environments, as Figure 1-4 illustrates. From a system perspective, this implies the following.

- ILE must support both the EPM and OPM exception-handling models.

- ILE must facilitate messaging (which differs in ILE from its predecessors) for all three models.

- ILE call support, which is certainly improved, must permit previous types of interprogram calling.

- ILE processes program parameters differently from OPM and EPM.

- ILE must support OPM and EPM program initialization, or startup, which is different in each of the three environments.

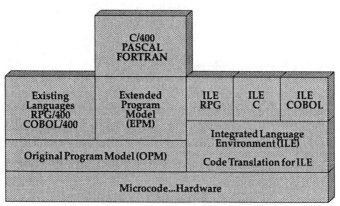

Figure 1 - 4: Example of an ILE RPG application in the OPM model

The features of procedural languages are better integrated into ILE than in its predecessors. In addition, enhancements to RPG give programmers tools they need for modular programming in a multilanguage environment. These tools include free-form expression, keyword definition, and a bound call operation, to name a few.

The ILE Solution

The ILE languages are ILE C/400, ILE RPG/400, and ILE COBOL/400. Certain programming languages are suited to particular task. The ILE model lets you use the most appropriate language for each task *within one application.*

The improved performance of call-intensive applications and improved applications based on appropriate mixed-language solutions, have their foundation in the common conceptual framework ILE provides for these languages. All ILE languages share the same model for storage management, exception handling, source-level debugging, improved system openness, and application component replacement.

Efficient Use of Runtime Storage

In terms of runtime storage space, ILE, unlike OPM and EPM, does not distinguish between programs in various languages. In contrast, consider an RPG program that performs an external call to a PL/I program under OPM and EPM. Not only does the system create a separate runtime environment for an initial external call to a PL/I program, but it creates a separate runtime environment for each subsequent call. If you have programmed in PL/I on the AS/400, you probably realize this is the reason why IBM introduced QPEICALL, which lets the system use an existing runtime call frame (remaining from previous calls to PL/I programs) rather than allocating and initializing new storage whenever a PL/I program is called externally from PL/I.

If each language in a multilanguage application insists on its own environment during execution, the result is inefficient use of system resources. To improve use of system resources, ILE can execute an entire application in a single runtime environment, if you so choose. The only stipulation is that the application consist of only ILE-language programs. (The system treats applications in mixed ILE and EPM environments differently.)

Consistent Error and Exception Handling

During program execution, various languages handle exceptions differently. For example, one language may handle a divide by zero by issuing a runtime error, whereas another language may handle a divide by zero by issuing a dump. Or different languages may have different ways for handling a square root of a negative number. Because the runtime of all ILE languages is built on the same base, you can depend on consistency in program behavior, especially in runtime message and exception management, program calling, parameter processing, screen handling, available programming services (such as math functions and date and time manipulation), and runtime performance.

You may be wondering how an inconsistency in error handling would manifest itself if you used languages not built on a common base or framework. Consider an example of two languages, where the first language has the following characteristics within its exception-handling model.

- You cannot provide your own exception handlers during program execution.

- The language does not implement program exceptions as interceptable messages; rather they are signals that invoke a default handler for a given program exception. The system cannot reroute the signal to another program that may be on the call stack at the time the exception occurs.

- The default handler gives you only one choice during program execution: to abort execution, at which point the entire application terminates, including all programs on the call stack.

Now, consider the characteristics of the exception-handling model for the second language in our example.

- This language supports user exception handlers. A program receiving an exception will first invoke any user exception handler before resorting to a default handler for the language.

- This language implements program exceptions as messages that the system may reroute to other programs on the call stack.

- The default handler for this language provides multiple choices: You may ignore the exception and resume execution at the next programmable instruction, abort the application, or retry the current programmable instruction.

This example of two types of languages illustrates how you would have to code differently if your application consisted of programs written in both of the above languages. The user might also be affected, as you might not be able to provide the same level of error handling, and therefore consistency, across the entire application interface as a result of the varying behavior and function in the languages in which that application was developed.

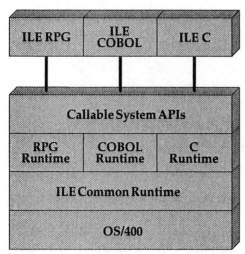

Figure 1 - 5: APIs available to ILE HLL programs

Migration

Because ILE supports procedural languages, applications written in this new environment should be much easier to port to and from other platforms. Porting and/or converting extremely large OPM/EPM application programs, some comprising well over 50,000 lines, to other, perhaps smaller, platforms would have been out of the question before ILE. ILE encourages a design and programming style that will yield applications that you can consider porting instead of rewriting.

Source-Level Debugging

ILE provides new debugging facilities that include features such as point-and-shoot display of field content without entering SEU. The STRDBG (Start Debug) command now begins a debugging session for both OPM/EPM and ILE programs.

Improved System Openness

The ILE model provides system interfaces by means of APIs (Application Programming Interfaces). These low-level functions let you manage storage, exceptions, and error conditions through system resources to which you would not ordinarily have access during runtime. The list in Figure 1-6 shows some examples of new APIs in ILE.

CEEDYWK	Calculates week day from given Julian date. This is one of many new date/time/timestamp functions available.
CEEHDLR	Lets you register a user-written condition handler. This set of APIs lets you work within and take advantage of ILE's error-handling architecture.
CEEHDLU	Unregisters a previously registered, user-written condition handler.
CEESxSNH	Computes hyperbolic sine.
CEESxCSH	Computes hyperbolic cosine.
CEEFRST	Frees storage.

Figure 1 - 6: Examples of ILE APIs

As Figure 1-5 shows, the system APIs are available to all high-level ILE source programs. Later, we will closely examine how application programs can use them.

Application Component Replacement

As we will explain later, service programs let you replace one component of the application without recompiling all programs that use that one component.

Conclusion

As this brief history demonstrates, ILE is the next step in the evolution of the AS/400's programming environment. Although ILE introduces new capabilities and functions to support mixed-language applications, this new environment also continues to support the OPM and EPM modules. As a result, you can develop new applications with modern programming methodologies, and your old programs will continue to work.

Before we get into our explanation of the details of ILE, we need a general overview of the differences between ILE programming and OPM/EPM programming. The next chapter will provide that overview by stepping through ILE program creation. In the course of this chapter, we will introduce the ILE concepts that will be the subject of the remainder of this book.

Creating an ILE Program

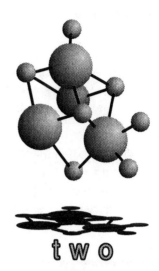

t w o

To set the stage for a detailed discussion of ILE program creation, it is helpful to review OPM program compilation. Then we can compare the new process for ILE program compilation.

The OPM example in Figure 2-1 consists of two source members, MAIN and TAX. Program MAIN will use an RPG CALL operation code to call program TAX, which computes Canadian federal and provincial tax amounts and returns to MAIN. The CALL operation code is a dynamic call, which means the system resolves the pointer to the called program during execution of the calling program.

The figure shows the steps required to compile and execute this application in the OPM environment. You execute the CRTRPGPGM command for each program to compile source members MAIN and TAX as separate executable programs. The result of each compile is an object of type *PGM.

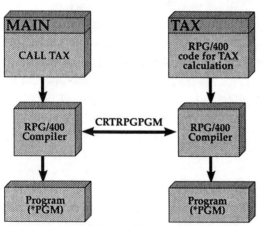

Figure 2 - 1: Example of an RPG application in the OPM model

The order of compilation in the OPM environment is irrelevant since MAIN issues a dynamic call to program TAX during runtime. The existence of TAX is not important to the compilation of source program MAIN because the system will resolve the pointer to TAX during execution, as is always the case with dynamic calling.

What's Different in ILE?

With this brief review of OPM program creation in mind, let's look at the two-step process of program creation in ILE. Figure 2-2 shows the same programming example as in Figure 2-1, except that now we are using the ILE RPG compiler.

In ILE, the program creation process is somewhat different from the one-step OPM process, in which you execute the CRTRPGPGM command to compile two executable programs, one of which calls the other. With ILE, you first execute the new CRTRPGMOD (Create RPG Module) command to compile two nonexecutable RPG program *modules*, both of which will be included in the final RPG program. Only after you execute the new CRTPGM (Create Program) command (the second step) will these modules become executable as part of the resulting *PGM object. Instead of *program* MAIN calling *program* TAX, *procedure* MAIN in *module* MAIN can call *procedure* TAX in *module* TAX. This call is via a new type of CALL operation code, the ILE RPG CALLB (CALL Bound) opcode, which we will discuss in due course. (Note that all ILE languages will provide specific syntax for bound calls.)

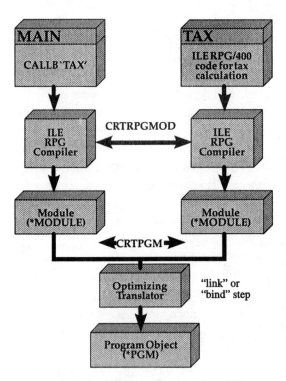

Figure 2 - 2: Example of an RPG application in ILE

Modules

Figure 2-2 shows ILE's new CRTRPGMOD command. You issue this command for each source member, MAIN and TAX, to invoke the ILE RPG compiler. This command produces nonexecutable module objects, which are object type *MODULE. Such objects are not executable entities until they go through the bind process (initiated through the CRTPGM command) that attaches them to and lets them execute as part of the *PGM object that results from CRTPGM.

This means that you cannot execute a *MODULE from the command line. You first have to bind your modules into a program object before you can run them.

If you have one module that constitutes your entire application, you follow the same steps. However, instead of CRTPGM, you may choose to use the CRTBNDxxx program command (xxx stands for the specific ILE language, for example, CRTBNDRPG for the RPG compiler). This command converts the single source object to *PGM. (Internally, CRTBNDxxx does create a module, but the compiler discards it after the compilation.)

Modules

*MODULE objects are analogous to OBJ files in DOS or OS/2. For example, in OS/2, if you use the C SET++ compiler, the output of the compiler is of type .OBJ. In the OS/2 environment, you compile all the different objects (which are like AS/400 modules, using ILE terminology), and then you use the linker (or binder, again using the ILE terminology) to glue all the objects together to get the .exe file (*PGM in ILE terminology). In ILE, you use the CRTPGM command to bind all modules together to get the *PGM executable object.

It's important not to confuse objects of type *MODULE with those of type *PGM. Remember, ILE *PGM objects are made up of one or more *MODULE object that you can reuse in multiple *PGM objects. Because of their reusability, modules are the basic building blocks of ILE programs.

Binding

As illustrated in Figure 2-2, after you have created *MODULE objects, you issue the new CRTPGM command to create an executable program object (*PGM) that contains both modules, MAIN and TAX. (In fact, in ILE, only two commands, CRTPGM and CRTBNDxxx, can create an executable program object.) You use a parameter of the CRTPGM command to list all the modules that comprise the application program. The CRTPGM command initiates a process that *statically binds* the specified modules together to produce an executable object of type *PGM.

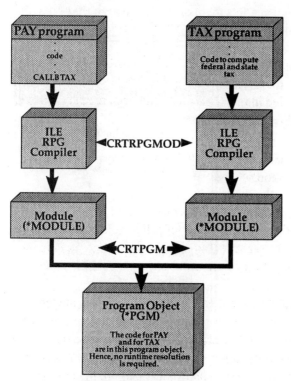

The term static binding is key to understanding the ILE model. Unlike the dynamic resolution for program calls in OPM, resolution for program calls in ILE is not restricted to runtime alone, but can occur when you issue the CRTPGM command. Resolution at this point is called *static*. *Binding* refers to gluing program modules together to form a single application. When you issue the CRTPGM command, the resulting bind step resolves all references and copies all the statically bound modules to the final executable object (i.e., the *PGM object).

Figure 2 - 3: ILE's bind-time resolution with the CALLB operation

Binding also identifies the main, or starting, entry point for the application. Given that your ILE application may contain more than one module, the operating system must know the main module to call first when you execute the OS/400 CALL command. Therefore, an entry point is required. The CRTPGM command has a parameter that identifies that point as the Program Entry Procedure (PEP).

In the C language, a module can consist of many functions, but it is the "main" function that gains execution control first when the program is called.

The distinction between OPM's runtime and ILE's bind-time resolution is important. (Figure 2-3 illustrates this distinction.) Runtime resolution for program objects is expensive in terms of performance, and facilitating static binds between procedures or global data items is a major contributor to the performance gains ILE provides. This is one way ILE can improve performance for call-intensive applications.

As Figure 2-3 shows, ILE uses a new call operation (CALLB — CALL Bound) from the PAY module. The new type of call is for calling procedures that are bound into the same *PGM object as the calling module. In contrast, an OPM CALL operation calls a different *PGM object.

The new call bound operation code is executed when you execute the CRTPGM command. ILE's binder locates the module that contains the TAX program and copies it into the *PGM as part of the binding process. As the figure shows, when the program executes, the code for the TAX module is part of the *PGM object, so no resolution is required. In contrast, with the OPM *dynamic call*, resolution of called programs must happen at runtime.

You use the CALLB operation code we have been talking about in a bound program. However, it's important to remember that this is not the only program type available in ILE.

ILE Program Types

As we've seen, the intention behind development of ILE was to promote modular programming techniques, without abandoning OPM and EPM legacy code and programming possibilities. Thus ILE supports three types of programs: unbound OPM programs, bound ILE programs, and ILE service programs.

1. *Unbound programs*: An unbound program is an OPM program that you've created outside ILE with a non-ILE compiler by using a CRTxxxPGM command. An unbound program does not include *MODULE objects. An example of an unbound program is an RPG/400 or COBOL/400 program that you have created with CRTxxxPGM and called from the OPM environment. Such programs contain a single entry point.

2. *Bound programs*: You create a bound program by using the CRTPGM or CRTBNDxxx command. Bound programs consist of one or more module objects (object type *MODULE) compiled with an ILE language compiler by means of a CRTxxxMOD command and bound together with CRTPGM. Figures 2-2 and 2-3 illustrate bound programs.

3. *Service programs*: A service program is a program of type *SRVPGM that you create with the CRTSRVPGM (Create Service Program) command. A service program is a collection of runnable procedures and available data items that other ILE programs or service programs can easily and directly access. In many respects, a service program is similar to a subroutine library or procedure library. Service programs provide services (e.g., communications or math routines) that several other ILE objects may need; hence the name service program. The chapter on service programs provides details.

Conclusion

ILE program creation requires two steps, as opposed to the one-step OPM process. In OPM, to create an executable *PGM object, you execute the CRTxxxPGM command that is appropriate for the HLL in which you've written your source code. In ILE, you first create nonexecutable *MODULE objects by executing the appropriate CRTxxxMOD command, and then you produce an executable object by issuing the CRTPGM command and binding the modules you want into the resulting *PGM object.

Modules are the building blocks that let you design efficient, refined applications that allow better performance than OPM programs. In addition, ILE encourages code reuse and improves maintainability through modules.

Because modules are the basic elements of ILE programming, understanding them is vital to understanding ILE. The next chapter explains modules and how they work in ILE.

ILE: A First Look

Modules

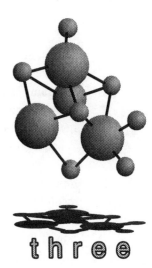

three

To achieve its mandate of code reusability and improved performance for mixed-language applications, ILE introduces a new type of AS/400 object, the *MODULE object. You can write the source for these independent, but nonexecutable, objects in any ILE language. You then use the respective CRTxxxMOD (e.g., CRTRPGMOD) command to compile *MODULE objects. When you've created all the modules you'll need for your application, you execute the new CRTPGM command, using a parameter to specify the modules you want the program to include. The result of CRTPGM is an executable program consisting of the specified modules.

Why Modules?

The purpose of *MODULE objects is to perform discrete tasks (similar to the tasks OPM programs perform) when an application calls procedures that are in modules within the application. Unlike OPM programs, however, ILE programs contain all the modules that contain the procedures that the program will call. Because modules are at the same time independent (although nonexecutable) objects and part of a *PGM object, the concept of modules is tied very closely to a two-step program-creation process. The first step is to create objects of type *MODULE. The second is to connect, or *bind*, together multiple *MODULES, such that one module can reference the procedures (or functions) and variables of others.

You may wonder why it is necessary to replace the OPM method of program creation. The explanation is straightforward: The new ILE method improves execution performance in applications that are call intensive.

As you are probably aware, calling from one program to another in OPM involves a search of the library list to resolve the reference to the called program. That is, during runtime, OS/400 must convert the called program's name to an actual storage location on the system. The criterion for this resolution by library search is the program name, or *symbol*. When a program references functions or procedures that reside in another program, the system can resolve these references either during runtime, as with OPM, or during compilation, as with ILE. During runtime, resolution is expensive in terms of performance as resolution is based on a *symbolic search* (i.e., a search by program name), which affects execution of the application. If resolution occurs during program creation, the execution performance of applications containing interprogram references improves greatly because no resolution occurs at runtime. For this reason, ILE's two-step program-creation process is vital to the development of efficient applications.

What Modules Contain

Modules can consist of one function or more, depending on the respective ILE language's syntax. For example, in ILE C, a source module can contain any number of functions, one of which may or may not be the main function. ILE RPG permits a single function per module, which corresponds to the mainline in a COBOL program or the main function in a C module. In RPG, each module is basically a standalone (but nonexecutable) program. This means each module has its own cycle, and when called, each module follows the RPG rules for initialization, execution, and termination.

When you are ready to use your modules within an application, you specify that particular modules will be part of the application by listing those modules on a parameter of the CRTPGM command. When you execute this command, the system copies the specified modules, resolves static binds, and creates an executable *PGM object.

Data Sharing

A major goal in developing ILE (as an enabler of modular programming) was to let application programs share data objects. Modules play an important role in achieving this goal because you specify whether data you define in a particular module will be available to other modules.

To understand data sharing in ILE, you need to understand the important concept of data declaration versus data definition. In simple terms, a program containing a *declaration* is indicating to the compiler that it will be using the declared item, which has been defined outside this, the declaring program. A program containing a *definition*, on the other hand, tells the system to set aside storage for the data item. When a program has defined data, that data is available for declaration in a different program.

Kernighan and Ritchie discuss the concept of data sharing in their book, *The C Programming Language*: "An external variable (i.e., a variable that can be accessed from another program or function) must be 'defined,' exactly once, outside of any function; this sets aside storage for it. The variable must also be 'declared' in each function that wants to access it; this states the type of the variable..." [Brian W. Kernighan and Dennis M. Ritchie, *The C Programming Language*, second edition, (Prentice Hall: Englewood Cliffs, NJ, 1988)].

An external variable is one other programs can access — READ or WRITE. For example, in C, you can use the "extern" language construct to externalize variables. FORTRAN uses COMMON to declare variables that are accessible outside the defining block. Until ILE, RPG did not provide a similar capability, nor was one necessary, given that RPG programs were single runtime entities. Now, with the ability to bind together more than one ILE RPG module, the need for sharing global, or external, fields becomes relevant.

IMPORT and EXPORT

To allow definition and declaration, ILE RPG now has Definition Specifications. These specifications let you specify that data in a defining module is available for EXPORT, and that a given module will IMPORT (or declare) data that has been defined in a different module.

To use the functionality of importing and exporting data in ILE RPG, you specify the new IMPORT and EXPORT keywords in the Definition Specification when you code a module. EXPORT indicates that this module allocates the storage for the field, but other modules in this application may use that storage. In ILE RPG, only one module in the application should define the field as EXPORT to ensure consistent runtime results. IMPORT indicates that you have defined the referenced data in another module that you will bind into the application.

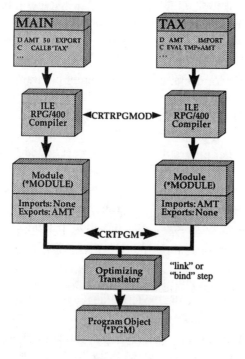

Figure 3 - 1: Modules with imports and exports

The reason for specifying that data will be available for export from a given module may appear more obvious than the reason for specifying that data will be available for import. The reason for IMPORT is that without import declaration, if a particular module contains references to variables or functions that are not defined within that module, an undefined variable error results during compilation.

When you define a particular data variable within a module, that module is called the defining module. The term declaring module refers to the module in which you declare or access that data. When you define a module with data that other modules within the application will use, that module (i.e., the defining module) is said to *export* the data. A bound module within the application (a declaring module) can then *import* that data by declaring it, and of course, the importing module must observe the type and attributes of that data as determined in the defining module.

Figure 3-1 shows the TAX application and this use of EXPORT and IMPORT. In this figure, TAX is the declaring module, so it must contain a Definition Specification that specifies that importing the program field AMT is allowed. main is the defining module, so it must contain the definition that sets aside storage for the program field AMT.

Module Information

In addition to declaring and defining data, modules contain information that the system can use to generate the executable program. For example, a module can contain a PEP (Program Entry Procedure), debug data, a UEP (User Entry Procedure), import and export specifications, and application code. Let's look at each of these pieces of information.

PEP (Program Entry Procedure): Because an application may now contain more than one module, the operating system must know which procedure is to receive control when you execute the OS/400 CALL command. To provide this information, you must specify an entry point into the program, the PEP. The CRTPGM command has a parameter that lets you identify a PEP. For example, the PEP specified for the *MODULE object display in Figure 3-2 is ROOT.

```
                          Display Module Information
Module . . . . . . . . . . . . :     ACCT_PAY
   Library . . . . . . . . . . :        TOPIWALA
Detail . . . . . . . . . . . . :     *BASIC
Module attribute . . . . . . . :

Module information:
   Module creation date/time . . . . . . . . . . . . . :   94/01/26 18:41:14
   Source file . . . . . . . . . . . . . . . . . . . . :   QRPGLESRC
      Library . . . . . . . . . . . . . . . . . . . . . :      TOPIWALA
   Source member . . . . . . . . . . . . . . . . . . . :   UTXSAN1
   Source file change date/time . . . . . . . . . . . :   93/12/03 15:34:28
   Owner . . . . . . . . . . . . . . . . . . . . . . . :   VDERPG
   Coded character set identifier . . . . . . . . . . :   65535
   Text description . . . . . . . . . . . . . . . . . :   Sanity test #1

   Machine instruction template included . . . . . . . :   *YES
   Sort sequence table . . . . . . . . . . . . . . . . :   *HEX
   Language identifier . . . . . . . . . . . . . . . . :   *JOBRUN
   Optimization level . . . . . . . . . . . . . . . . :   *NONE
   Maximum optimization level . . . . . . . . . . . . :   *FULL
   Debug data . . . . . . . . . . . . . . . . . . . . :   *NO
   Compressed . . . . . . . . . . . . . . . . . . . . :   *NO

   Program entry procedure name . . . . . . . . . . . :   ROOT
   Number of parameters . . . . . . . . . . . . . . . :   0          255
   Module state . . . . . . . . . . . . . . . . . . . :   *USER
   Module domain . . . . . . . . . . . . . . . . . . . :   *SYSTEM
   Number of exported defined symbols . . . . . . . . :   1
   Number of imported (unresolved) symbols . . . . . . :   13

Module compatibility:
   Module created on . . . . . . . . . . . . . . . . . :   V3R1M0
   Module created for . . . . . . . . . . . . . . . . :   V2R3M0
   Earliest release module can be restored to . . . . :   V2R3M0
```

Figure 3 - 2: Display module information panel

You can think of the PEP as a compiler-generated branch point within an
ILE program. The PEP actually functions as nothing more than a label to
which execution control goes upon program startup. It is a "procedure"
in the sense that it gains execution control, pulls parameters off the command line, and then branches to the User Entry Procedure (UEP). Each
language determines how the user-written procedure is to get control.
For C, the only modules that can have a PEP are those that have a main
procedure. When you select the module with the PEP procedure (via
CRTPGM), then the PEP knows that when it comes time to call the user-
written procedure, it is the main procedure in this module object. For
RPG, since there is only one procedure per module, each module object

contains a PEP. When the module with the PEP is identified (via CRTPGM), then the user-written procedure in that module is the procedure to get control when the PEP has finished.

A PEP is optional (depending on the language) for each module because you define multiple modules to create a single program, and only one needs to have an entry point defined. From an ILE point of view, a module does not have to contain a PEP. In the case of RPG, a PEP is not optional, whereas for C, only the module with the main procedure contains a PEP. In Figure 3-3, a PEP has not been defined.

UEP (User Entry Procedure): This user-written procedure is the target of a dynamic call. The UEP is the procedure in your program that you want to execute as the result of a call, and this procedure actually gets control from the PEP. In C, the UEP is the main function that would gain execution control from the PEP after program startup. In Figure 3-3, the UEP is defined to be procedure ACCT_PAY.

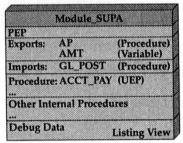

Figure 3 - 3: Contents of a module

Debug Data: The compiler generates all debugging data necessary for debugging a running ILE object. You specify that you want debug data as an optional parameter of the create command (i.e., CRTxxxMOD, CRTBNDxxx, CRTSRVPGM, or CRTPGM). The debug data value essentially indicates the type of view that will be visible if you execute a program containing the module in debug mode. This topic is discussed in detail in the chapter on the ILE debugger.

Exports: When you specify that something in a given module is available for export, you indicate which data items and/or procedures are visible outside the scope of the module object. Two items are exported by module SUPA in Figure 3-3: AP, which is a procedure, and the variable, AMT.

Imports: When you specify that this module will import something, you indicate which data items and/or procedures this module will reference that have been defined in another module that will be bound with this one in a *PGM object. The imported item for module SUPA in Figure 3-3 is the procedure, GL_POST.

Application Code: This is the actual code that you write for the application. It can be in ILE C, COBOL, or RPG.

Conclusion

Modules are the building blocks of ILE programs. Modules contain the functions and data items necessary for the program as well as the information the system needs to generate an executable program. In addition, because an ILE application contains the modules it will call to perform particular tasks, the performance of these applications is much better than similar OPM programs that must call other programs.

This chapter has shown what modules are, why they are important to ILE, and what they contain. But to really understand modules and how they work in ILE programs, you have to understand the way ILE ties modules together to form an executable program object. That process is called binding, and the next chapter will examine binding in detail.

Binding

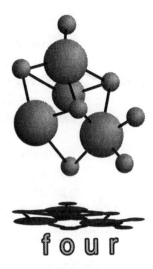

Because modules are independent, nonexecutable objects that you want to use in various executable programs, you need a way to specify which *MODULE objects belong to which application or program. In ILE, the means of specifying these modules is the CRTPGM command. CRTPGM has a parameter that lists the modules you want to attach to the *PGM object that is the result of executing CRTPGM. This command initiates a process called *binding*, which is what copies the specified modules in to this *PGM object. Because modules are copied into the program object, any change to a module after program creation will *not* affect the program.

What is Binding?

One formal definition of binding is "to associate an absolute or virtual address with a symbolic address or label in a program which corresponds to storage or an executable function or procedure within a program." This definition is clearer if you understand that the absolute (and virtual) address refers to a variable, program name, or entry point within a called program. The reference may be as simple as a name, label, or (as is possible with C) a pointer to a function. And, whatever the representation, it must be resolved to an actual, physical storage location.

This definition and explanation apply to any environment that provides a mechanism for binding multiple components to produce a single application. This chapter will specifically explain binding with respect to ILE.

In ILE terms, binding is a mechanism for linking multiple program components (modules) to produce a single application. When you create a *PGM-type object, you specify which modules you want to bind together to form the application. The term *bound module* refers to the individual modules that together make up an application of type *PGM.

In other words, binding associates multiple modules with each other, bringing them together to form a single, executable program of object type *PGM. The CRTPGM command achieves this goal by activating the binder.

Dynamic Binding and Static Binding

ILE provides two types of binding: dynamic and static binding. If a program object consists of modules bound together as a result of executing CRTPGM, that program is statically bound. You can use the RPG CALLB (a static, or bound call) operation code to call bound modules.

If a program object does not contain modules (e.g., an OPM program compiled with CRTRPGPGM), that program is dynamically bound to a called program when you issue the RPG CALL operation code. During program execution, dynamic binding provides references (pointers) to the separate programs that make up the application. This is the type of binding OPM supports. Dynamic binding does not produce actual copies of the individual modules that will eventually comprise the resulting application. Rather, dynamic binding supplies a pointer to each of those modules. During execution, the system resolves this pointer to a physical address.

In summary, the two types of binding in ILE are dynamic and static. With dynamic binding, all resolution happens at runtime. This is the method used today with all OPM compilers. Static binding can be done by two methods, bind by copy and bind by reference. With bind by copy, the system physically copies all modules into the application that will use them. With bind by reference, the system statically binds to a service program (*SRVPGM object) that has an export that is needed.

Which Type of Binding Is Better?

Each method of binding has its advantages and disadvantages. A key concern with dynamic binding is the time necessary to resolve addresses during execution. A key concern with static binding is the size of the resulting application. With these considerations in mind, let's examine the characteristics that make an application a good candidate for dynamic bind and the characteristics that suit an application for static bind.

First, dynamic bind is a good solution if the modules are large (because resolution occurs only once), or if the application consists mainly of modules that infrequently reference functions and variables outside themselves so that minimal resolution is required during execution.

When considering which type of binding to use, you must weigh module size and available storage on the system against how frequently the modules access variables and functions or procedures contained in other modules.

An application is a good candidate for static binding if the purpose of each module is unique, and if few application programs use a particular module.

When determining if an application is a good candidate for static binding, consider whether different application programs on the system frequently use each module. If 40 different applications on the system use a module, ACCOUNTS_PAY, which is 5Mb in size, you will have 40 applications times 5Mb which equals 200Mb of copies on the complete system. If storage is a concern, you should consider dynamic binding or service programs. If the typical module in your application is as large as ACCOUNTS_PAY but only two applications use it, storage may not be a great concern (i.e., 2 applications times 5Mb equals 10Mb). This example can be more impressive if the applications that use ACCOUNTS_PAY very rarely access variables or functions defined in ACCOUNTS_PAY. This translates into inefficient use of storage merely to satisfy a few references. Here, you should definitely consider dynamic binding.

You can see why bind by reference may be a more appropriate choice for such an application. But let's make that point even clearer by looking again at the familiar TAX application, shown in Figure 4-1, to illustrate good use of bind by copy.

Figure 4-1 shows the two-step program creation ILE requires. In the first step you execute the CRTxxxMOD command. The second is the binding step, which you initiate with the CRTPGM command. The bind step creates a linkage between modules MAIN and TAX making it possible for module MAIN to call module TAX.

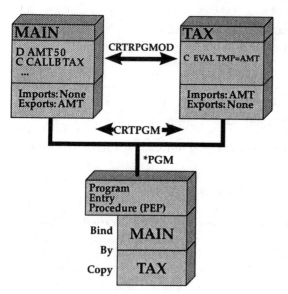

Figure 4 - 1: Bind by copy

Under a one-step program creation process, as with OPM, you're probably familiar with the fact that the program you are calling doesn't have to exist on the system while you are compiling the program that performs the call. The called program has to exist only when you run the calling program. The two-step compilation process, as with ILE, lets you reference subroutines (which ILE replaces with modules) that will be resolved during the second step, the bind step, which ties all the modules into one application. In contrast to the situation with the one-step creation, the binder will issue an error if a called module is missing at bind time.

In the example in Figure 4-1, TAX accesses a variable, AMT, that resides in the source module containing the MAIN program. The import and export lists associated with each program establish the access to the variable AMT. The *export list* associated with the MAIN program indicates to the compiler that other programs bound with MAIN can access a variable AMT. The *import list* associated with TAX indicates to the compiler that although TAX contains no definition for the variable AMT, this variable will be resolved during bind time. Otherwise, as you can imagine, an error for the undeclared variable AMT would occur.

With service programs, you specify an export list on the EXPORT parameter of the CRTSRVPGM command. The *ALL value specifies export for all procedures and variables. The *SRCFILE value indicates that binder source has been provided. To specify an import list, you must use your HLL's construct for importing a data item (i.e., a variable or function name). For example, in C, you use the *extern* keyword, and in RPG, you use the new Definition Specifications. Importing a data item is the same as declaring it. To export a data item, you must already have defined it.

Finally, note that the resulting program object (type *PGM) contains copies of MAIN and TAX because this object is the result of bind by copy. In contrast, if we had chosen bind by reference, the result would be pointers to the called program TAX from MAIN. These pointers would be resolved during runtime. In bind by copy, this resolution occurs at bind time.

To illustrate dynamic bind, let's look at Figure 4-2. This figure shows the same example using the dynamic bind technique.

In contrast to the bind-by-copy version of TAX, this version does not require that the application program contain copies of programs MAIN and TAX. Rather, the application contains the names of program(s) to be called and necessary data items, and these references are resolved at runtime. When the system encounters a call to a program from the module currently being executed, the system will search the library list for a program of that name. Upon finding the name, the system will activate the procedure. This activation is more expensive than binding the module containing the called procedure to the calling program. The reference to a program requires much less storage than the actual program, so, given that TAX and MAIN are large modules, this solution is more storage efficient. As with bind by copy, you must weigh the storage savings against call frequency to make the appropriate choice.

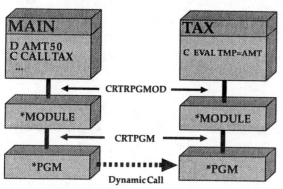

Figure 4 - 2: Dynamic binding

Conclusion

ILE requires a two-step program creation process. First, you create nonexecutable *MODULE objects. Then, you create a *PGM object that includes whatever *MODULE objects you need. The CRTPGM command initiates the process that attaches modules to a program, and this process is called binding.

If modules are the building blocks of ILE, binding is the mortar that holds those blocks together. Out of these building blocks and mortar, you can construct programs. In addition, you can assemble another structure, a *service program*. The next chapter explains service programs and their function.

ILE: A First Look

Service Programs

Now that we've discussed the concept of *MODULE objects, we can introduce a new structure into the ILE program creation process: the service program. A service program is a bound program that consists of *MODULE objects and that you compile with the CRTSRVPGM command. The resulting object of type *SRVPGM provides a collection of runnable procedures and data items that other ILE programs or service programs can easily and directly access by means of a call. We cannot call service programs directly from the command line. Rather, they are tools that other programs and service programs use. These objects provide services that several other ILE objects may need; hence the name service program.

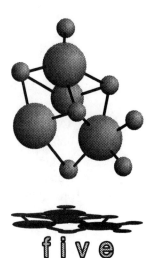

What Is a Service Program?

In many respects, a service program is similar to a subroutine library or procedure library. Service programs let you export one (or multiple) function or procedure and variable into a *PGM object at one time. In other words, you need not develop one module per function you want to make available for use in multiple *PGM objects. Instead, you can put multiple functions into one service program. Rather than binding individual modules into a *PGM object, you bind several modules into a service program by executing CRTSRVPGM, and then you bind the service program into a *PGM object by executing CRTPGM.

You should consider collecting modules in a service program when you specifically write modules that will provide the same services to multiple applications on the system. If, for example, you worked for an insurance company, you could write the various routines that calculate earned premium, unearned premium, and rate and then bind them into a service program that many of your applications could access.

To create a service program, you can use any module or group of modules. That is, the modules that will comprise a service program are not special. You can use the same modules you incorporate in your *PGM objects. In fact, if you use certain routines in several programs, you will probably want to recompile these routines as modules that you will bind together to produce service programs. This approach will improve access and maintenance methods for those programs and help you deal with their growing usage.

Why Service Programs?

What can service programs offer that *PGM objects cannot? The answer is that service programs 1) give you individual protected interfaces for specific modules, 2) allow multiple program entry points, and 3) can reduce program size. Let's look at what each of these characteristics of service programs means.

Protected Interfaces

Unlike objects of type *MODULE, service programs let you *externalize*, or make visible to users, only the functions that you want exposed. You may, for example, have a service program that provides the following functions.

- CALCULATE_FEDERAL_TAX

- CALCULATE_PROVINCIAL_TAX

- CALCULATE_TAX

You could externalize CALCULATE_FEDERAL_TAX and CALCULATE_PRO-VINCIAL_TAX but hide CALCULATE_TAX.

Multiple Entry Points

Service programs can contain more than one externalized entry point, or callable function. To help you understand the implications of this characteristic, consider C program FRED that contains many functions, none of which are mainline. If you want to access FRED's capabilities, you don't access just one function that is designated as the entry point; you can access as many routines as FRED's developers have externalized. Most important, FRED does not contain a mainline. It is a collection of individual routines that perform specific functions. This concept maps very closely to the idea of DLLs in OS/2.

Size

Programs consisting of bound *MODULE objects are larger than programs using service programs that contain the same function. The reason is that CRTPGM does not bind *SRVPGM objects into the program in the same way as it binds *MODULE objects. Unlike *PGM objects, service program objects are activated and loaded into memory once per activation group (i.e., the ILE program execution environment: The system creates an activation group before execution and awards the activation group all the necessary resources to execute that program, including dynamic, static, and automatic storage — see Chapter 7 for detailed information about program and service program activation). Because of binding, calling a procedure in a service program is faster and more efficient than a dynamic call to a *PGM object.

Service Program Example

We can bring home these points by looking at an example of a general-ledger posting, or GL_POST, module in an accounting package. Figure 5-1 outlines module GL_POST.

Let's begin with how to bind this module into a program. Assume that steps 0 through 8 in GL_POST are internal functions or procedures (or sub-routines for ILE RPG). You need an object of type *PGM containing module GL_POST. And you want to bind the *MODULE objects (i.e., AR, AP, and AJ) that use GL_POST together with GL_POST so that these modules can access GL_POST's POST entry point. POST is the only callable entry point within this module because steps 0 through 8 are internal to GL_POST and have no value on their own.

Figure 5-2 shows the CRTPGM command screen with the values filled in for creating the AP program, which includes module GL_POST.

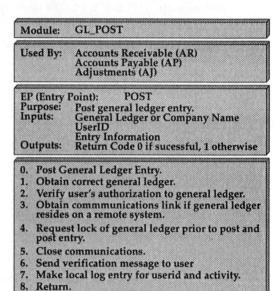

Module:	GL_POST

Used By:	Accounts Receivable (AR) Accounts Payable (AP) Adjustments (AJ)

EP (Entry Point):	POST
Purpose:	Post general ledger entry.
Inputs:	General Ledger or Company Name UserID Entry Information
Outputs:	Return Code 0 if sucessful, 1 otherwise

0. Post General Ledger Entry.
1. Obtain correct general ledger.
2. Verify user's authorization to general ledger.
3. Obtain commmunications link if general ledger resides on a remote system.
4. Request lock of general ledger prior to post and post entry.
5. Close communications.
6. Send verification message to user
7. Make local log entry for userid and activity.
8. Return.

Figure 5 - 1: Example of routine that is used by multiple applications

```
                          Create Program (CRTPGM)
Type choices, press Enter.

Program . . . . . . . . . . . .   AP            Name
   Library . . . . . . . . . . .   CAROL         Name, *CURLIB
Module . . . . . . . . . . . . .   AP            Name, generic*, *PGM, *ALL
   Library . . . . . . . . . . .   CAROL         Name, *LIBL, *CURLIB...
             + for more values   GL_POST
                                 CAROL
Text 'description' . . . . . . .   'Accounts Payables'

                          Additional Parameters

Program entry procedure module   *FIRST         Name, *ONLY, *FIRST
   Library . . . . . . . . . . .                 Name, *LIBL, *CURLIB...

Bind service program . . . . . .   *NONE         Name, generic*, *NONE, *ALL
   Library . . . . . . . . . . .                 Name, *LIBL
             + for more values

Binding directory . . . . . . .   *NONE         Name, *NONE
   Library . . . . . . . . . . .                 Name, *LIBL, *CURLIB...
             + for more values

Activation group . . . . . . . .   *NEW          Name, *NEW, *CALLER
Creation options . . . . . . . .                 *GEN, *NOGEN, *NODUPPROC...
             + for more values
Listing detail . . . . . . . . .   *NONE         *NONE, *BASIC, *EXTENDED...
Allow Update . . . . . . . . . .   *YES          *YES, *NO
User profile . . . . . . . . . .   *USER         *USER, *OWNER
Replace program . . . . . . . .   *YES          *YES, *NO
Authority . . . . . . . . . . .   *LIBCRTAUT     Name, *LIBCRTAUT, *CHANGE...
```

Figure 5 - 2: Creating program AP and binding module GL_POST

As Figure 5-2 shows, the accounts payable program we're creating includes the GL_POST module and the AP module. Both modules reside in library CAROL. CRTPGM's program entry procedure module parameter indicates which module (in this case, AP) will gain execution control first when the program is called.

Within the AP program, module GL_POST includes a call to the POST routine. This program structure works, but we must realize that we are exposing the developers of AP, AR, and AJ to a lot of code within GL_POST (e.g., routine 5, Close Communications) that they need not be bothered with and perhaps should not have access to.

A Service Program

To improve this situation, let's consider a change — not to the function of GL_POST but to the way in which we will provide the POST service to the developers of AR, AP, and AJ. We need a way to provide the POST service and only the POST service. That is to say, we want to secure all internal routines. To achieve this goal, we can create an object of type *SRVPGM. The screen in Figure 5-3 shows the CRTPGM command with a service program specified instead of individual modules.

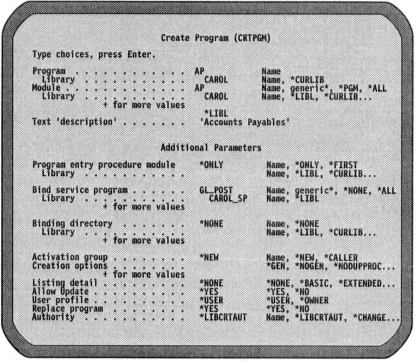

```
                            Create Program (CRTPGM)

Type choices, press Enter.

Program . . . . . . . . . . .   AP              Name
  Library . . . . . . . . . .     CAROL         Name, *CURLIB
Module . . . . . . . . . . . .   AP              Name, generic*, *PGM, *ALL
  Library . . . . . . . . . .     CAROL         Name, *LIBL, *CURLIB...
            + for more values
                                *LIBL
Text 'description' . . . . . .   'Accounts Payables'


                         Additional Parameters

Program entry procedure module   *ONLY          Name, *ONLY, *FIRST
  Library . . . . . . . . . . .                 Name, *LIBL, *CURLIB...

Bind service program . . . . .   GL_POST        Name, generic*, *NONE, *ALL
  Library . . . . . . . . . .     CAROL_SP      Name, *LIBL
            + for more values

Binding directory . . . . . .   *NONE           Name, *NONE
  Library . . . . . . . . . .                   Name, *LIBL, *CURLIB...
            + for more values

Activation group . . . . . . .   *NEW           Name, *NEW, *CALLER
Creation options . . . . . . .                  *GEN, *NOGEN, *NODUPPROC...
            + for more values
Listing detail . . . . . . . .   *NONE          *NONE, *BASIC, *EXTENDED...
Allow Update . . . . . . . . .   *YES           *YES, *NO
User profile . . . . . . . . .   *USER          *USER, *OWNER
Replace program . . . . . . .    *YES           *YES, *NO
Authority . . . . . . . . . .    *LIBCRTAUT     Name, *LIBCRTAUT, *CHANGE...
```

Figure 5 - 3: Creating program AP with GL_POST as a service module

Notice that GL_POST no longer appears as a module to be bound with the
AP module for the creation of the AP program. We've moved GL_POST
into the bind service program parameter. Of course, this means that
GL_POST is no longer an object of type *MODULE. It is now object type
*SRVPGM. Figure 5-4 shows how we created the GL_POST service pro-
gram.

```
                    Create Service Program (CRTSRVPGM)

 Type choices, press Enter.

 Service program . . . . . . . .   GL_POST      Name
   Library . . . . . . . . . . .   CAROL_SP     Name, *CURLIB
 Module . . . . . . . . . . . . .  GL_POST      Name, generic*, *SRVPGM, *ALL
   Library . . . . . . . . . . .   CAROL        Name, *LIBL, *CURLIB...
              + for more values

 Export . . . . . . . . . . . . .  *SRCFILE     *SRCFILE, *ALL
 Export source file . . . . . . .  QSRVSRC      Name, QSRVSRC
   Library . . . . . . . . . . .   CAROL_SP     Name, *LIBL, *CURLIB
 Export source member . . . . . .  GL_EXP       Name, *SRVPGM
 Text 'description' . . . . . . .  'Service Program - GL_POST'

                                                                   Bottom


 F3=Exit   F4=Prompt   F5=Refresh   F10=Additional parameters   F12=Cancel
 F13=How to use this display        F24=More keys
```

Figure 5 - 4: Creating a service program

Before specifying that the GL_POST service program is in library
CAROL_SP, we created a GL_POST object of type *MODULE in library
CAROL. Then we executed the CRTSRVPGM command, binding module
GL_POST into this new service program. The service program and the
module we used to create it have the same name. This overlap in names
is possible because the two are of different object types, *SRVPGM and
*MODULE.

ILE Binder Language

Because we want to provide security and not expose all the code in GL_POST, an interesting parameter on the CRTSRVPGM panel is *Export*. This parameter indicates which functions, procedures, and data items you want to externalize. It lets you secure individual functions within the service program. In the *Export source file* parameter, you can specify a member of a source file to determine whether it should or should not be exported. If a certain function in your service program contains sensitive data, you can specify that that function is not eligible for export.

During service program creation, you specify the library, file, and member in which that member resides. In Figure 5-4, we see that the export source physical file specified is QSRVSRC. The type of that member is BND, and in our example, it is in library CAROL_SP.

To indicate which procedures and data items will be externalized from the service program that you are creating, ILE provides a new language, the ILE *binder language*. The binder language consists of the following commands:

STRPGMEXP (Start Program Export) command, which identifies the beginning of a list of exports from a service program.

EXPORT (Export Symbol) command, which identifies a symbol name (i.e., in our example, a function name) available to be exported from a service program.

ENDPGMEXP (End Program Export) command, which identifies the end of a list of exports from a service program.

A program you write with the binder language is called binder source. You can use the export parameter to specify the binder source file you want to use for this service program. Figure 5-5 contains the binder source for the GL_EXP member.

Note that binder source is not compulsory. If you want to externalize all entry points and variables in the service program, the export parameter accepts a value of *ALL rather than *SRCFILE, thereby eliminating the need for a binder source to define individual modules for export.

```
Columns . . . :    1  71              Browse                    CAROL_SP/QSRVSRC
SEU==>                                                             _  GL_EXP
FMT **   ...+... 1 ...+... 2 ...+... 3 ...+... 4 ...+... 5 ...+... 6 ...+... 7
         *************** Beginning of data ********************************************
0001.00 STRPGMEXP PGMLVL(*CURRENT) LVLCHK(*YES)
0002.00    EXPORT SYMBOL('POST')
0003.00 ENDPGMEXP
         *************** End of data ****************************************
```

```
F3=Exit   F5=Refresh   F9=Retrieve   F10=Cursor   F12=Cancel
F16=Repeat find         F24=More keys
```

Figure 5 - 5: Binder source

In Figure 5-5, the second line of the source member, EXPORT SYM-BOL('POST'), is the exports list, which shows that POST is the function being exported, or externalized. STRPGMEXP and ENDPGMEXP delimit the exports list. (You may export multiple items from a service program by adding entries to the exports list, i.e., by adding EXPORT SYMBOL entries.) This exports list serves a dual function: 1) It indicates which items (functions, procedures, variables) are being externalized, and 2) it defines this service program's *public interface* (i.e., provides the names of the service program's exported variables, functions, procedures). In addition, the exports list determines the signature value.

Signatures

The *signature* is a non-zero, system-generated value based on the order and context of the STRPGMEXP – ENDPGMEXP block (i.e., the public interface) in the binder source. The system generates one signature value for each public interface defined by a STRPGMEXP – ENDPGMEXP block. The purpose of a signature is to verify that a program that references a particular service program is using a valid public interface. The binder matches the referencing program's signature value against the service program's signature values. If a match exists, the program may use the service program without being recompiled. It is important to note that the signature does *not* validate the interface to a particular procedure or function in a service program, but to the entire service program.

You can define multiple exports lists (public interfaces) by specifying multiple STRPGMEXP – ENDPGMEXP blocks. However, only one such list may have a value of *CURRENT on the PGMLVL parameter of STRPGMEXP. Other public interfaces in the same binder source must have a value of *PRV for PGMLVL.

To disable signature checking, you specify a value of *NO for the LVLCHK parameter of STRPGMEXP for a particular public interface. This value generates a zero value. A *YES value generates a non-zero value and enables level checking.

You need not specify level checking if one of the following conditions exists: 1) you are sure that changes to the interface will never cause incompatibilities, 2) you do not want to update the binder source, or 3) you do not want to recompile applications that use the service program.

Binding Your Service Program to the Application

Let's review the steps for creating the AP program that uses the GL_POST service program.

1) Issue the CRTRPGMOD (Create RPG Module) command to create any required module objects.

2) Issue the CRTSRVPGM (Create Service Program) command, binding together the modules you created in step 1, to create the service program. The resulting service program is object type *SRVPGM. It is important to note that you have created the service program at this point, and a third step is necessary to bind the service program to the ILE application program. By performing the following step, you allow applications to use the newly created service program.

3) Issue the CRTPGM command to bind all non-service program application modules together with the service program created in Step 2 above. The resulting object type is *PGM.

Note that service program modules can have debug data associated with them. You compile your service program modules with debug information for maintenance purposes (see the chapter on debugging for details about how to specify debugging).

Conclusion

Service programs are an excellent vehicle for delivering reusable function while providing security for individual components of the service program and minimizing maintenance. Like a subroutine or procedure library, a service program lets you export one or multiple functions or procedures and variables in a program object at one time. Additional advantages of service programs are that they may have multiple entry points and that they can reduce your program size.

To selectively export data items and procedures or functions from a service program, you can use the new binder language. The binder source you create in the binder language defines a service program's public interface. As an alternative to binder source, you can specify that everything in the service program is exportable. To do this you use the EXPORT parameter of CRTSRVPGM.

Because service programs can include a large number of modules, ILE provides a tool that lets you quickly and easily specify the modules you want to use. This tool is called a binding directory. The next chapter will introduce and explain binding directories and then step through an example program that puts together everything we've covered so far.

Binding Directories

So far, you see that an ILE program object is the result of a two-step process: compiling and creating. You first compile the various source programs to create modules, and then you bind all the parts (*MODULE as well as *SRVPGM objects), using the CRTPGM command, to create an executable *PGM object.

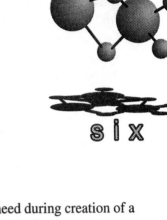

To facilitate this process, ILE introduces another function: *binding directories*. Binding directories are system objects of type *BNDDIR. These objects contain the names of modules and service programs that you may need during creation of a program or service program. You may think of binding directories as containers that can have entries for names of modules and service programs to let you specify just the directory at CRTPGM time. With a binding directory, you don't have to list all modules and service programs you want included each time you create a new program object. The system simply searches the binding directory for the objects needed at bind time.

What Binding Directories Do

Recall from our earlier discussion of binding that ILE resolves external procedure names and data items during the binding step of program creation. If you have specified a binding directory and the program you are creating has an import request (this can be a procedure or variable name) that is unresolved at bind time, the system checks the modules in the binding directory. If the binding directory contains the name of a *MODULE or *SRVPGM object and that object contains an export that satisfies an unresolved import request in the program you are creating, the system will bind by copy to the module that contains the export and by reference if the export is found in a service program. In other words, the binding directory facility gives the binder the physical address of the required procedure or data item.

Recall from the chapter on service program creation that CRTSRVPGM, like CRTPGM, has a parameter in which you list the modules you want to use in that creation. Binding directories are an alternative to this list on both CRTSRVPGM and CRTPGM.

A binding directory is just a list of modules and service programs. Looking inside a binding directory, for each entry in the directory, you would find the information shown in Figure 6-1.

Object Name	Name of module, service program
Object Type	For example, *SRVPGM or *MODULE
Library	Name of the library in which the listed object resides

Figure 6 - 1: Information in a binding directory

The objects listed do not have to exist on the system during creation of the binding directory. However, they must exist when you execute CRTPGM or CRTSRVPGM.

Creating a Binding Directory

You create binding directories with the CRTBNDDIR (Create Binding Directory) command. Figure 6-2 shows CRTBNDDIR's parameters.

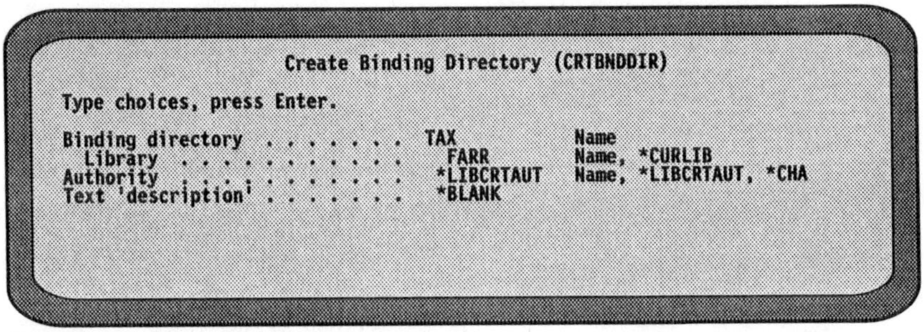

```
                 Create Binding Directory (CRTBNDDIR)

 Type choices, press Enter.

 Binding directory  . . . . . .   TAX           Name
      Library  . . . . . . . . .      FARR       Name, *CURLIB
 Authority  . . . . . . . . . .      *LIBCRTAUT  Name, *LIBCRTAUT, *CHA
 Text 'description'  . . . . . .   *BLANK
```

Figure 6 - 2: CRTBNDDIR command

This command's only mandatory parameter is the name of the directory. In this example, we create a directory to contain all modules and service programs that deal with tax manipulations. This way, if we create any application that might require any of the service programs or modules in this directory, we can simply specify this directory name on the CRTPGM command when we create this new application.

To add entries (i.e., modules and service programs) to our binding directory, we use the ADDBNDDIRE (Add Binding Directory Entry) command. Figure 6-3 displays ADDBNDDIRE's parameters.

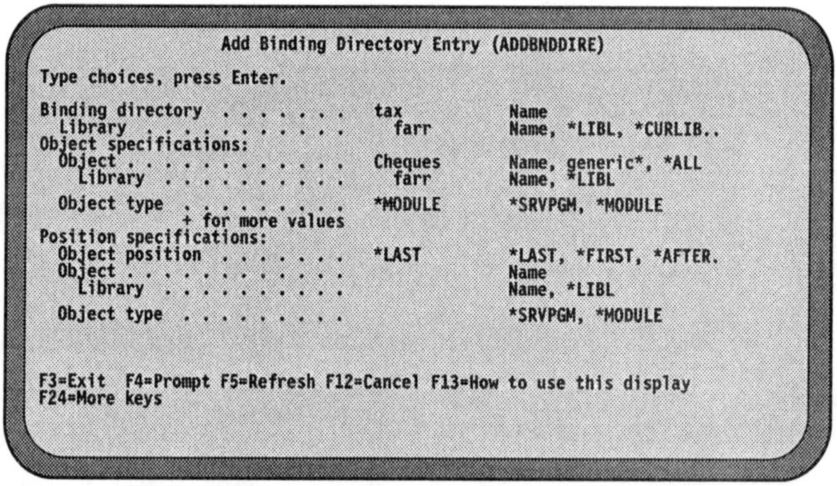

```
                 Add Binding Directory Entry (ADDBNDDIRE)

Type choices, press Enter.

Binding directory . . . . . . .   tax          Name
    Library . . . . . . . . . .   farr         Name, *LIBL, *CURLIB..
Object specifications:
    Object . . . . . . . . . . .  Cheques      Name, generic*, *ALL
    Library . . . . . . . . . .   farr         Name, *LIBL
    Object type . . . . . . . .   *MODULE      *SRVPGM, *MODULE
                  + for more values
Position specifications:
    Object position . . . . . .   *LAST        *LAST, *FIRST, *AFTER.
    Object . . . . . . . . . . .               Name
    Library . . . . . . . . . .               Name, *LIBL
    Object type . . . . . . . .                *SRVPGM, *MODULE


F3=Exit  F4=Prompt F5=Refresh F12=Cancel F13=How to use this display
F24=More keys
```

Figure 6 - 3: ADDBNDDIRE command

In this command, we specify the binding directory name and the list of modules and service programs we want to add to this directory. These commands are not the only ones of interest when we're using binding directories.

CL Commands Associated with Binding Directories

To let you work with the new functions ILE provides, IBM has added several new CL commands. Figure 6-4 lists the new CL commands for use with binding directories.

Command	Description
CRTBNDDIR	Create a binding directory
DSPBNDDIR	Display a binding directory
ADDBNDDIRE	Add a binding directory entry to the specified binding directory
RMVBNDDIRE	Remove a binding directory entry from the specified binding directory
DLTBNDDIR	Delete a binding directory
WRKBNDDIR	Work with a binding directory
WRKBNDDIRE	Work with a binding directory entry

Figure 6 - 4: Binding directory commands

From a development perspective, binding directories are useful for organizing your battery of favorite modules. They help you keep all these required modules under one umbrella. Although binding directories are useful, please keep in mind that they are a matter of convenience and nothing more. There is nothing that you can do with a binding directory that you cannot achieve otherwise.

It is important to note that there is a difference in the output generated (*PGM) when you use binding directories versus using only the module parameter on the CRTPGM/CRTSRVPGM commands. If *MODULE objects are specified on the module parameter of the CRTPGM/CRTSRVPGM commands, those modules will be bound by copy whether or not they are used. If a module is in a binding directory, it gets bound by copy only if it is needed.

Putting It All Together

So far we have been talking about programs, service programs, and binding directories, but we have treated them all independently. To glue all the pieces together, we would like to show an example that uses modules, binding directories, and service programs.

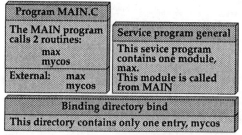

Figure 6 - 5: Overview: modules, service programs, and binding directories

First, let's look at the overview in Figure 6-5 and describe the example we'll be walking through. In this example, we have a main program that calls two different functions, max and mycos. max returns a maximum of two numbers, and mycos returns the cosine of a number. We create module max and bind it to a service program, whereas we create module mycos and add it to a binding directory by using the ADDBNDDIRE command.

Throughout this discussion, note that we chose this example to show how programs, binding directories, and service program fit together, so we intentionally made these functions as simple as possible to direct your attention away from the code itself. As a result, the service program and binding directory contain only one module each. In reality, of course, each would contain multiple modules and other service programs, or they wouldn't serve much purpose.

In the following sections, we will cover all the steps necessary to input the source code, create a module, create a binding directory, and create a

service program. We used ILE C for this example, but you can use any
ILE language.

Creating the Source

To start, we have to create a main program and two different functions.
Figure 6-6 is the source for the main program.

```
SEU==>
FMT **  (...+... 1 ...+... 2 ...+... 3 ...+... 4 ...+... 5 ...+... 6 ...
*************** Beginning of data ****************************
0001.00 #include    <stdio.h>
0002.00 #include    <ctype.h>
0003.00
0004.00 extern int    max(int, int);
0005.00 extern double mycos(double);
0006.00
0007.00 int main(int argc, char * argv%>[])
0008.00 {
0009.00     int    result, five, six;
0010.00     double num;
0011.00
0012.00     five=5;
0013.00     six=6;
0014.00
0015.00     result=max(five,six);
0016.00     printf ("The max number is -->%d\n",result);
0017.00
0018.00     num=mycos(25.0);
0019.00     printf ("cosine of 25.0 is -->%f",num);
0020.00 }
**************** End of data ****************************
```

Figure 6 - 6: Source code for main

The very simple main program uses two different functions, max and
mycos: max to find the maximum value of two fields and mycos to return
the cosine of the number 25. At the top of the code, to tell the compiler
that these functions are not in this source member, we declare max and
mycos as external. The compiler just generates the code it sees here and
leaves it up to the binder to find these external routines. Figure 6-7 displays the two different functions main uses.

```
SEU==> _____
FMT ** (...+... 1 ...+... 2 ...+... 3 ...+... 4 ...+... 5 ...+... 6 .
       ***************** Beginning of data *****************************
0001.00 /*****************************************************************
0002.00 /* Function max compares 2 integer values and rtn the largest
0003.00 /*****************************************************************
0004.00
0005.00 int max(int x, int y)
0006.00 {
0007.00
0008.00    if (x>y)
0009.00       return (x);
0010.00    else
0011.00       return (y);
0012.00 }
       ***************** End of data ****************************
SEU==> _____
FMT ** (...+... 1 ...+... 2 ...+... 3 ...+... 4 ...+... 5 ...+... 6 .
       ***************** Beginning of data *****************************
0001.00 /*****************************************************************
0002.00 /*         Mycos returns a cos of a number of type double.
0003.00 /*****************************************************************
0004.00 double mycos(double x)
0005.00 {
0006.00    return cos(x);
0007.00 }
       ***************** End of data ****************************
```

Figure 6 - 7: Source code for max and mycos

Creating the Modules

Now, we call the compiler and create *MODULE objects for all three
source members. Figure 6-8 shows the CRTCMOD command parameters
for main.

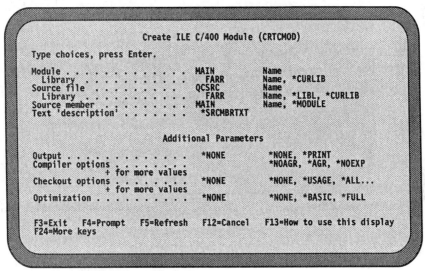

```
                      Create ILE C/400 Module (CRTCMOD)

Type choices, press Enter.

Module . . . . . . . . . . . .   MAIN          Name
    Library . . . . . . . . .    FARR          Name, *CURLIB
Source file . . . . . . . . .    QCSRC         Name
    Library . . . . . . . . .    FARR          Name, *LIBL, *CURLIB
Source member . . . . . . . .    MAIN          Name, *MODULE
Text 'description' . . . . . .    *SRCMBRTXT


                         Additional Parameters

Output . . . . . . . . . . . .   *NONE         *NONE, *PRINT
Compiler options . . . . . . .                 *NOAGR, *AGR, *NOEXP
           + for more values
Checkout options . . . . . . .   *NONE         *NONE, *USAGE, *ALL...
           + for more values
Optimization . . . . . . . . .   *NONE         *NONE, *BASIC, *FULL


F3=Exit   F4=Prompt   F5=Refresh   F12=Cancel   F13=How to use this display
F24=More keys
```

Figure 6 - 8: Calling the ILE C/400 compiler

We execute the CRTCMOD command for all three source members, main,
mycos, and max. The result of this step is the creation of three modules of
object type *MODULE.

Creating a Binding Directory with an Entry

Now that we have created the modules, we want to first create a binding directory to contain an entry for module mycos. (Don't forget that this example is simplified and that a binding directory would ordinarily contain entries for numerous modules and/or service programs.) Figure 6-9 shows the CRTBNDDIR command parameters for main.

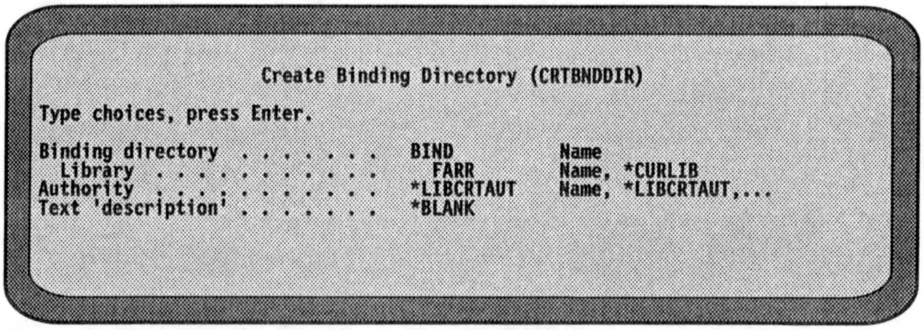

```
                    Create Binding Directory (CRTBNDDIR)
Type choices, press Enter.

Binding directory  . . . . . . .   BIND        Name
   Library  . . . . . . . . . . .     FARR      Name, *CURLIB
Authority  . . . . . . . . . . .   *LIBCRTAUT  Name, *LIBCRTAUT,...
Text 'description' . . . . . . .   *BLANK
```

Figure 6 - 9: Creating a binding directory CRTBNDDIR

Pick any name for a binding directory. In our example, we call it BIND. Now that we have created the directory, we can add modules to it using the ADDBNDDIRE command, as in Figure 6-10. In this example, we add the function mycos to the directory.

```
          Add Binding Directory Entry (ADDBNDDIRE)
Type choices, press Enter.

Binding directory . . . . . .   BIND        Name
  Library . . . . . . . . . .   FARR        Name, *LIBL, *CURLIB...
Object specifications:
  Object . . . . . . . . . .    MYCOS       Name, generic*, *ALL
    Library . . . . . . . . .   FARR        Name, *LIBL
  Object type . . . . . . . .   *MODULE     *SRVPGM, *MODULE
                + for more values
Position specifications:
  Object position . . . . . .   *LAST       *LAST, *FIRST, *AFTER...
  Object . . . . . . . . . . .              Name
    Library . . . . . . . . .               Name, *LIBL
  Object type . . . . . . . .               *SRVPGM, *MODULE



F3=Exit  F4=Prompt  F5=Refresh  F12=Cancel  F13=How to use this display
F24=More keys
```

Figure 6 - 10: Adding an entry to a binding directory

As you can see, this command requires you to specify only the binding
directory name and then list all the modules you want entered in the directory. Notice that you may have modules and/or service programs in
this directory.

In addition to CRTBNDDIR and ADDBNDDIRE, ILE introduces a few commands that you can use with binding directories. For example, you can
specify DLTBNDDIRE (Delete Binding Directory Entry) to remove an entry from a directory. See Appendix A for a list of commands you can use
with binding directories.

Creating a Service Program

The next step in this example, is to create a service program to contain the second function, max. Figure 6-11 illustrates this step by showing the CRTSRVPGM command.

```
                    Create Service Program (CRTSRVPGM)
Type choices, press Enter.

Service program  . . . . . . .   GENERAL         Name
  Library  . . . . . . . . . .     FARR          Name, *CURLIB
Module . . . . . . . . . . . .   MAX             Name, generic*....
  Library  . . . . . . . . . .     FARR          Name, *LIBL, *CURLIB...
              + for more values
                                 *LIBL
Export . . . . . . . . . . . .   *ALL            *SRCFILE, *ALL
Export source file . . . . . .   QSRVSRC         Name, QSRVSRC
  Library  . . . . . . . . . .     FARR          Name, *LIBL, *CURLIB
Export source member . . . . .   EXPORT          Name, *SRVPGM
Text 'description' . . . . . .   *BLANK


                           Additional Parameters

Listing detail . . . . . . . .   *FULL           *NONE, *BASIC, ...


F3=Exit F4=Prompt F5=Refresh F10=Additional parameters  F12=Cancel
F13=How to use this display      F24=More keys
```

Figure 6 - 11: Creating a service program (CRTSRVPGM)

In this example, since we have only one function in the module, (which is, as we've said, unusual for a service program), we specified *ALL on the export parameter. This allows all functions to be exported out of the service program. In this case, we are exporting the max function.

As we've seen, another way to specify what functions are exportable is by using the ILE binder language, which is a small set of nonrunnable commands. You enter binder-language commands in a source member, just as you enter C or RPG source code. (The binder language also enables a source-entry syntax checker to prompt and validate the input

when you specify a BND source type.) Figure 6-12 shows an example
of the source statements you might enter in a source member as an
alternative to the *ALL option on the *export* parameter of CRTPGM or
CRTSRVPGM.

```
Columns . . . :    1  71              Browse              FARR/QSRVSRC
SEU==>
FMT **  ...+... 1 ...+... 2 ...+... 3 ...+... 4 ...+... 5 ...+... 6 .
        *************** Beginning of data ****************************
0001.00 STRPGMEXP PGMLVL(*CURRENT) LVLCHK(*YES)
0002.00     EXPORT SYMBOL('max')
0003.00 ENDPGMEXP
```

Figure 6 - 12: Binder language source

To indicate to the system that you are using a binder-language source
member to describe all your exports, enter SCRFILE on the export parameter of the CRTSRVPGM command and also specify the file, library,
and member.

Creating the Program

So far, we have created a binding directory, a service program, and all the modules. We can now execute the final step to glue everything together and produce a runnable *PGM object. Figure 6-13 shows the CRTPGM command with the parameters we specified.

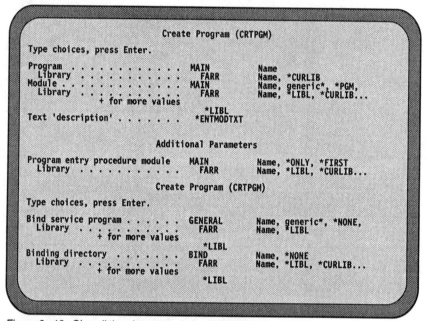

Figure 6 - 13: Glue all the pieces together with CRTPGM

In the *Program entry procedure* parameter, we specified that main is the first entry that should be called. This means the function main will execute first when we call this program.

main will be the entry to the program. Of course, we have to specify the name of the binding directory in which mycos has an entry and the service program to which max is bound. When we execute the CALL command, the binder will resolve all references.

To tie everything together, you can display what the final program object (*PGM) includes by executing the DSPPGM (FARR/MAIN) command. This command will display two modules that are bound by copy and one service program that is bound by reference.

Conclusion

Binding is ILE's tool for gluing together the constituent parts of a program, and ILE provides alternative ways to do that for various situations. You can simply bind modules in as many different *PGM objects as you like. Or you can bind modules into a service program and, in turn, bind the service program into a *PGM. To facilitate binding several modules (and/or service programs) into a program, ILE provides binding directories, which provide the system with a list of modules and service programs for resolving imports.

The vehicle for starting the binding process is the create (CRT) command you execute to create the program object. That command gives the system all the information it needs. But the names of the program's constituent parts are not the only information the system needs. In addition to the parameters of CRTPGM that specify module and service program names or the binding directory name, there is one more parameter of that command that we have not yet discussed. That parameter determines the program activation environment by letting you specify an activation group.

Because ILE *PGM objects are different from OPM/EPM programs, a new program activation model was necessary for ILE. The next chapter discusses program activation.

ILE: A First Look

Program Activation

From a user's perspective, starting an ILE program implies nothing more than calling the executable program object from the command line or performing a call operation within a program. In fact, of course, these actions cause a great deal to take place. This chapter explains the events that occur during program startup in ILE.

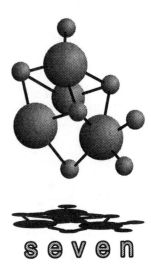

seven

What Are Activation Groups?

Before executing an ILE application, the system determines all the resources that will be necessary to execute that program. These resources are dynamic, static, and automatic storage, including the executable program, extra storage for execution, temporary data management resources, exception handlers, and ending procedures for program termination. Then, only for the purpose and duration of this program's execution, the system creates an environment that allocates all these resources. This environment, within which an ILE program is executed, is called an *activation group*.

You can think of the activation group as an OS/400 substructure that comes into existence only for the execution of a program. This substructure determines how the program is activated and deactivated, how open files are handled during program termination, and how exceptions are signaled and handled.

So far, we've been talking about one program executing in one activation group. However, an application can consist of multiple programs, and AS/400 applications run in jobs, which can include multiple applications.

So, in the ILE program activation model, an activation group lets you execute multiple programs and service programs, and a job can have multiple activation groups executing at any moment. Because a job can have its own activation group, the job can manage resources without worrying about conflicts with other jobs executing in different activation groups. Once execution is complete, the system usually cleans up the activation group, and it disappears.

Figure 7-1 illustrates ILE's program activation structure. In the figure, Job X includes Activation Group X_1, in which Program A executes, and the same job includes Activation Group X_2, in which Program D and Program B execute. The programs that are active within an activation group behave cooperatively as an application. But an application may activate multiple activation groups. So Figure 7-1 shows Activation Group X_2 in Job X with both Program D and Program B executing. Similarly, Activation Group Y_1 in Job Y has Program B and Program C, and other activation groups are part of Job Y, as well. This arrangement illustrates the primary function of activation groups: to let unrelated applications, such as packages from different vendors, have their own environment in the same job and thus avoid resource conflicts.

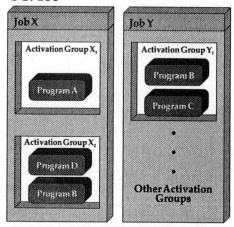

Figure 7 - 1: ILE's activation structure

Within an activation group, a program is activated when you issue a call to a procedure or function within a module that is bound into that program. Once a program is activated, that program uses some of the resources allocated at the job level for its execution. A program is activated only once per activation group. That is, when a program is activated, any further calls to that program will not activate that program again. Consider Figure 7-2, which shows how resources are allocated to an activation group as programs are activated.

The figure is an execution snapshot of a job containing Activation Group A. After initialization, Program X is called (that is, some procedure or function in some module bound to that program has been called), and the system makes a call-stack entry X. Because the call stack is a last-in, first-out (LIFO) structure and Program X is the first program called, the call-stack entry for X is at the bottom of the stack. In contrast, the activation group's list of active programs shows X at the top because X is the first program activated.

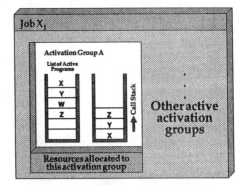

Figure 7 - 2: How resources are allocated to an activation group

Next, program Y is called. Likewise, the system makes a call-stack entry for Y on top of X and adds Y to the list of active programs below X. At this point, neither X nor Y has returned to its calling program.

Now, assume that Y calls a program W, which performs its tasks and returns to its caller, Y. The system puts W into the list of active programs below Y, makes a call-stack entry for W, and then removes the call-stack entry when W returns to its caller. As shown in the figure, although W no longer appears in the call stack, W has been activated, so it remains active. It is important to note here that W remains active although no call-stack entry exists at the moment of this execution snapshot. After the return from the call to W, program Y calls Z. The system enters Z into the call stack above Y and into the list of active programs below W.

In summary, once a program is activated, it remains activated until the activation group is deleted. As a result of this rule, it is possible to have active programs, such as program W in the example, that are not on the call stack but remain active in the activation group until the activation group is deleted. With this understanding, we can move on to discuss how to specify which activation group a program belongs to.

Activation-Group Specification

You use the ACTGRP parameter of the CRTPGM or CRTSRVPGM command to indicate which activation group a program will execute in. Figure 7-3 shows the CRTPGM command screen with the ACTGRP parameter filled in.

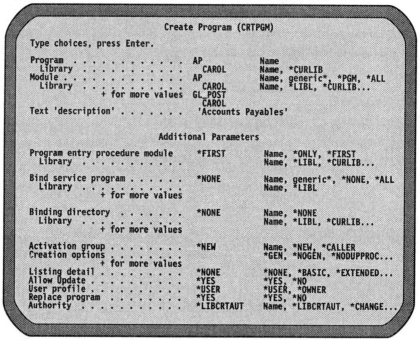

```
                          Create Program (CRTPGM)

Type choices, press Enter.

Program . . . . . . . . . . . . .   AP            Name
  Library . . . . . . . . . . . .     CAROL       Name, *CURLIB
Module . . . . . . . . . . . . .    AP            Name, generic*, *PGM, *ALL
  Library . . . . . . . . . . . .     CAROL       Name, *LIBL, *CURLIB...
              + for more values     GL_POST
                                    CAROL
Text 'description' . . . . . . .    'Accounts Payables'


                          Additional Parameters

Program entry procedure module      *FIRST        Name, *ONLY, *FIRST
  Library . . . . . . . . . . . .                 Name, *LIBL, *CURLIB...

Bind service program . . . . . .    *NONE         Name, generic*, *NONE, *ALL
  Library . . . . . . . . . . . .                 Name, *LIBL
              + for more values

Binding directory . . . . . . .     *NONE         Name, *NONE
  Library . . . . . . . . . . . .                 Name, *LIBL, *CURLIB...
              + for more values

Activation group . . . . . . . .    *NEW          Name, *NEW, *CALLER
Creation options . . . . . . . .                  *GEN, *NOGEN, *NODUPPROC...
              + for more values
Listing detail . . . . . . . . .    *NONE         *NONE, *BASIC, *EXTENDED...
Allow Update . . . . . . . . . .    *YES          *YES, *NO
User profile . . . . . . . . . .    *USER         *USER, *OWNER
Replace program . . . . . . . .     *YES          *YES, *NO
Authority . . . . . . . . . . . .   *LIBCRTAUT    Name, *LIBCRTAUT, *CHANGE...
```

Figure 7 - 3: CRTPGM command screen with the ACTGRP parameter

The acceptable values for ACTGRP are a user-named activation group, a system-named activation group, or the name of the calling program's activation group. Let's examine each choice.

A User-Named Activation Group

You can create multiple programs that will execute within the same activation group by specifying a name of your choice on the ACTGRP parameter when you create each program. When you provide the name of an activation group, the system creates that activation group on demand. By specifying the programs that will execute in particular activation groups, you have the power to manage applications at an activation-group level. This is beneficial, for example, to software developers because they can select different activation groups for different applications to isolate their programs from other software developers' applications running under the same job.

A System-Named Activation Group

If you specify the *NEW value for the activation group parameter, the system will create a new activation group whenever this program is called. ILE will choose the name for the activation group, and it will be unique to the job in which that program will execute. ILE will verify that there is no naming conflict with user-named activation groups active within that same job. As soon as you leave this program, the activation group created for it disappears.

The Calling Program's Activation Group

Specifying *CALLER tells the system to use the calling program's activation group. In other words, this option tells the system that when this program is called, the program should be activated into the caller's activation group. When you specify this parameter value, the system will never create a new activation group for the execution of the program.

You must specify one of these activation group parameters for ILE programs and service programs. The reason is that when a job starts, the system creates two default activation groups: One will be used for the execution of OS/400 system code and the other for the execution of OPM programs. ILE programs may not execute within the default OPM activation group unless the ILE program or service program was created with the *CALLER value on the ACTGRP parameter, or the call to the ILE program or service program originated from an OPM program. And, of course, an ILE program may not execute in the activation group for system code. Because ILE programs are not allowed in either of these activation groups, you must specify an activation group.

Activation-Group Management

The user-named activation group value is a very important one for activation-group management, which means controlling which activation groups your programs will execute in. As mentioned in the discussion of this parameter value, managing activation groups is important for developers who want to isolate their applications. It also becomes important as the number of activation groups on your system grows: You can leave activation group proliferation up to the system, but you'll probably find it's more efficient to determine yourself what programs run in what activation groups. Figure 7-4 illustrates how you can organize an application by providing your own

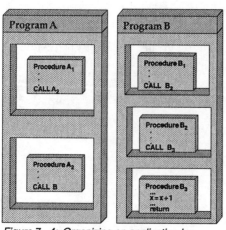

Figure 7 - 4: Organizing an application by activation group

activation group names as you create your programs. This application includes two programs, A and B. Program A contains procedures A1 and A2. Program B contains procedures B1, B2, and B3.

The screens in Figures 7-5 and 7-6 show the CRTPGM commands used to create programs A and B. Note the *Activation group* parameter for each command. For program A, we specified the user-defined name of AG_A. On the activation group parameter for program B, we specified the user-defined name of AG_B. In this way, we can control which programs (thereby which procedures and functions) are executed in which activation groups.

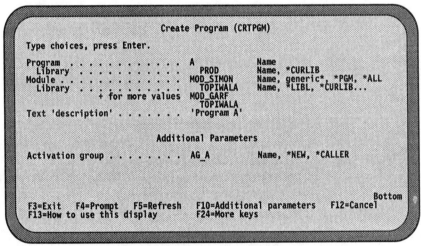

Figure 7 - 5: Specifying activation group AG_A for program A

```
                        Create Program (CRTPGM)
Type choices, press Enter.

Program . . . . . . . . . . . .  B              Name
  Library . . . . . . . . . . .    PROD         Name, *CURLIB
Module . . . . . . . . . . . . .  MOD_NAT       Name, generic*, *PGM, *ALL
  Library . . . . . . . . . . .    TOPIWALA     Name, *LIBL, *CURLIB...
                                  MOD_KING
                                  TOPIWALA
              + for more values  MOD_COLE
                                  TOPIWALA
Text 'description' . . . . . . .  'Program B'


                        Additional Parameters

Activation group . . . . . . . .  AG_B          Name, *NEW, *CALLER


                                                              Bottom
F3=Exit   F4=Prompt   F5=Refresh   F10=Additional parameters   F12=Cancel
F13=How to use this display        F24=More keys
```

Figure 7 - 6: Specifying activation group AG_B for program B

From Figure 7-4, we can assume the following call flow.

```
    A1 calls
    – A2 calls
        – program B ...

    B1 calls
    – B2 calls
        – B3
```

When procedure B3 is called, while the statement $x = x + 1$ in procedure B3 is executing, the execution environment could be depicted as in Figure 7-7.

When procedure A1 is called, the system creates activation group AG_A because we specified the user-defined activation group name parameter on CRTPGM. Procedure A1 is called and entered as a call stack entry.

Next, procedure A2 is called and entered on the call stack. Program B is called. Before execution control is given over to procedure B1 in program B, the job allocates a new activation group called AG_B, as we specified on the activation group parameter of CRTPGM. After B1 is entered on the call stack, B2 and B3 are called.

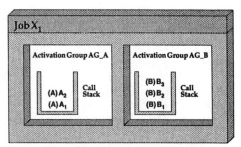

Figure 7 - 7: Execution environment of Job X1 when procedure B3 is called

Having covered what an activation group is and how to specify and manage one, we can now look at what an activation group comprises. Then we can examine what actually happens during activation.

Contents of an Activation Group

A main characteristic of activation groups is that they share resources across the job, so OS/400 allocates storage for activation groups at the job level. Let's look more closely at what an activation group contains and how the system allocates storage.

You already know that a job can contain more than one activation group. Each activation group in a job must contain system resources necessary for the execution of that activation group's programs. In addition, each activation group must contain its own call stack, temporary data management resources, a list of active programs, and exception handlers. Figure 7-8 shows the contents of each activation group in a job.

The storage for an activation group may be static, automatic, or dynamic. Program variables that will be retained between procedure calls are placed in static storage. Program variables that do not retain their values between program calls are placed in automatic storage. Dynamic storage

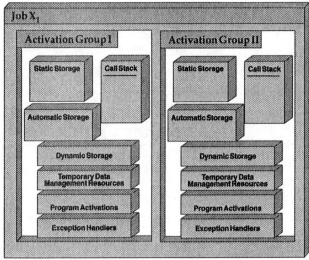

Figure 7 - 8: Contents of activation groups within a job

satisfies any memory allocation (that is, extra storage requested by the executing program).

It is important to note here that the system protects the storage for each activation group executing within a job. That is, a "runaway pointer" in a C program executing in Activation Group I should not affect the storage allocated to Activation Group II. If storage integrity is an issue with your applications, your design should provide separate activation groups for the high-risk programs.

As Figure 7-8 shows, the system gives every activation group its own call stack, indicating which programs are currently executing within that activation group. The programs in the call stack are in a nonreturn state, and not all programs have to be executing. Some programs may be active but not executing. All activated programs are contained in the program activation, as shown in the figure.

The temporary data management resources depicted in Figure 7-8 refer to the following items. These are the resources required for the execution of AS/400 programs that use any database or communications facility.

- Pointers to any open files the applications are currently using
- Commitment definitions
- Local SQL cursors
- Remote SQL cursors
- Hierarchical file system
- User Interface Manager
- Query Management services
- Open communication links
- Common Programming Interface communications

Finally, each activation group contains its own set of exception handlers. Exception and condition handlers are discussed in the chapter on the ILE exception model.

Knowing what activation groups contain makes it fairly easy to infer what happens during program activation. The next section completes the picture.

Program Activation

During activation, or program load, the system performs four steps.

1. The system uses an explicit library/program name or the library list to locate the program.

2. Then the system allocates required static storage for the program being called. More than one job can execute a program (or service program), and it is the activation process that ensures that each job has its own copy of storage to prevent it from violating the storage of another job that may be executing at the same time. A program can be assured the same level of storage integrity within a job that has multiple activations executing that program.

3. Next the system initializes storage.

4. Finally, the system completes resolution of external references. (External references are data items or procedure names that are imported from other modules.) During program creation, with the program, the system saves a table containing a list of these external references. The system then converts these symbolic references to actual physical storage addresses for use during execution.

Remember that if the program has already been called once within the same activation group, the system will not reactivate it. An activated program remains activated until the system destroys the activation group.

As with all OS/400 objects, multiple applications may share ILE programs running concurrently in different jobs. If a particular program is executing more than one job, each job, and consequently each program, maintains its own private copies of any program variables and functions.

Consider this diagram, which shows multiple jobs concurrently using a payroll application. Each program using PAYROLL receives an independent execution space for PAYROLL within that using program's activation group. For example, when program User(A) calls program PAYROLL, the activation group for User(A)'s program activation allocates, manages, and initializes static storage for program variables and fields from PAYROLL. Because each job has its own execution-time storage space, if PAYROLL contains a variable, TAX, 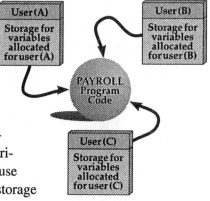 each of the three jobs calling PAYROLL can set that variable to a different value. You can imagine the disastrous possibilities if two concurrent pro-

grams were sharing the same static storage and each program were un-
aware that other jobs were sharing the space it was accessing.

Service-Program Activation

In addition to these program activation steps, service programs have
unique steps for activation. These steps are as follows.

1. *Start-up*: When the system calls an ILE program that is bound
   (by reference) to a service program, that service program is activated as part of that call by reference. Also, if that service program is bound by reference to other service programs, they too
   are activated.

2. *Binding*: Service-program activation completes the interprogram binding linkages. Symbolic links are converted to physical links.

3. *Signature checking*: The system checks signatures for level
   checking.

The steps that are important to know about here are checking for
binding and signature checking, which we explained in the chapter on
service programs.

For any ILE program activated for the first time within an activation
group, the system checks for binding to any service programs. If the program being activated has calls to service programs, these service programs are activated as part of the same call. The process is repeated for
each service program in the application program until all necessary service programs are activated.

The signature, which you use for level checking, is a binder-generated
number determined by the order of procedure names and data-item
names contained in the exports list within a service program's binder

source. In the binder source, the STRPGMEXP and ENDPGMEXP pair delim-
its an exports list, and if you specify level checking, the signature is
matched during activation-time to verify that this service program still
supports the same exports list.

Conclusion

ILE activation groups let you determine the environment in which each of
your programs will run so that you can prevent accidental resource conflicts with other applications. Activation groups give your applications
new possibilities for managing resources (e.g., open files and active programs) within a job.

At this point, we've covered all the basic elements of ILE: program creation, modules, binding, service programs, binding directories, and program activation. Now, we can explore some additional aspects of ILE that
provide interesting capabilities. The next chapter will introduce some
new APIs that we can bind into ILE programs to get functionality that
would otherwise be unavailable. The following chapter will explain exception handling and some new capabilities available with ILE. Then
things get really interesting as we examine the new ILE source-level debugger and step through some examples. Finally, we'll give you the questions and answers that come up most frequently when we talk to users
about ILE.

APIs

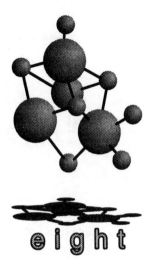

APIs (Application Programming Interfaces) are programs or functions that an
operating system supplies to provide access to specific system-level data or
function that is not otherwise readily
available to HLL programs. Programmers have been using APIs since the ear-
liest operating systems, but only
recently have APIs become known to
AS/400 HLL programmers. In the early
days of the AS/400, little internal technical documentation for low-machine-
level data and functions was available. But responding to growing demand for access to such system data and function, IBM introduced callable system APIs in OS/400 V1R3.0. This high-powered tool set lets you
harness important system functionality, such as obtaining and freeing system storage or obtaining system date and time information.

What Do APIs Do?

Although wide availability of APIs is relatively new to AS/400 HLL programming, some AS/400 APIs have been around for a long time. For example, you may not have realized that a call to QCMDEXC is an API call (IBM
identifies all available callable system APIs by prefixing them with the
letter Q). To illustrate the use of APIs, let's look at a program fragment
that uses QCMDEXC.

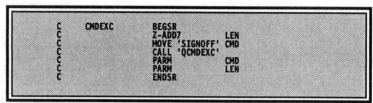

Figure 8 - 1: Code fragment using the QCMDEXC API

In Figure 8-1, the program fragment checks for status value 1331 to verify that a timeout has occurred. If a timeout has occurred, the QCMDEXC API signs off the device. In Figure 8-1, QCMDEXC has two parameters: the command you want it to execute, in this case SIGNOFF, and the command's length.

As another example of how APIs can be useful, imagine that you need date and time information in a program. New system APIs allow access to and manipulation of such data. Without these APIs, you would have to write code to get the date and time — that is, provided they are available to your HLL to begin with.

Before V1R3.0, OS/400 offered several APIs in addition to QCMDEXC. Figure 8-2 shows some of these other APIs and explains their functions.

API	Description
QDCXLATE	Use a system translation table to translate individual fields
QSYSTRNTBL	Translates upper- to lowercase and vice versa.
QCLSCAN	Scan for a string pattern
QCMDCHK	Verify syntax of a CL command string
QSNDDTAQ	Send a text to a given data queue
QRCVDTAQ	Receive text from a data queue

Figure 8 - 2: Pre-Version 1, Release 3.0 APIs

Version 1, Release 3.0 APIs and Concepts

With APIs in V1R3.0, IBM introduced two important concepts. First, objects known to the operating system belong to one of two domains, *SYSTEM or *USER. All IBM-supplied objects and those created during execution belong to the *SYSTEM domain. User-created programs are *USER domain objects. Second, any executing program must be in one of these two domains. The domain controls which objects your programs can access and what types of actions you may perform on those objects through APIs.

When IBM provided increased access to AS/400 APIs, a new security configuration became necessary to protect *SYSTEM domain programs and data. Without this new security, inappropriate use of some APIs could have affected system integrity. The solution was to introduce security level 40 for compiling programs with *SYSTEM and *USER domains. You can use security level 40, or you can waive it from the system.

When a user is executing application programs, security level 40 restricts the user to the *USER domain and prohibits access to *SYSTEM domain programs or data except via APIs. You can call APIs from application programs executing in *USER domain to access objects in the *SYSTEM domain.

Figure 8-3 lists some APIs that IBM provided for OS/400 V1R3.0. (For a comprehensive list, see the *System Programmer's Interface Guide (SC21-8223)*.) Before V1R3.0, such low-level functionality was available only through MI (Machine Interface). As you can see, IBM modeled these R3.0 API names after CL command names.

API	Description
QPRCRTPG	Create a program from MI source
QUSLOBJ	List objects to a user space
QUSPTRUS	Retrieve a pointer to the beginning of a user space
QQXMAIN	Execute a Query Manager function
QREXQ	Manipulate a REXX queue
QUSCRTUQ	Create a user queue

Figure 8-3: Version 1, Release 3.0 APIs

Although V1R3.0 provided a limited number of APIs, they were a beginning to a very important movement, system openness. In Version 2 R3.0, ILE is clearly following this trend towards openness, taking advantage of a much richer and more powerful set of system APIs for use with your ILE high-level programs.

Benefits of APIs

Of the many reasons that illustrate the importance and benefit of using APIs to access system function and data, four are predominant. APIs provide protection, are available through external calls, are upward compatible, and improve performance.

1. *Protection*: Using system APIs protects both the operating system and the user. From the operating system perspective, one way to shield vital or critical system objects from users is by not providing API access to such objects. From the user's perspective, APIs guarantee that applications on the system's runtime will not violate program space that a particular application is using.

2. *External Calls*: APIs are accessible through an external call, which is available in all HLLs. In the case of RPG, you would use a CALL operation code. Parameter lists communicate the information being referenced and, in some cases, changed.

3. *Upward Compatibility*: APIs insulate you from changes that may occur at the operating-system or machine level. If you access system routines through MI without using APIs, you have no protection against possible changes in the operating system that might affect your code. And if you want to take advantage of added system function, IBM can provide more APIs with future releases of the operating system.

4. *Performance*: Because APIs give you a direct line of communication with the system, you get improved performance.

APIs in ILE

Although OS/400 V1R3 provided some APIs to access system objects, much of OS/400's function was still unavailable to user programs. V1R3 and the introduction of ILE and the ILE programming languages have enlarged the set of APIs and increased the range of functions available to your HLL programs.

Not only does ILE make new APIs available, but the concept of binding lets you easily include APIs in your HLL programs. The list below shows the areas in which binding APIs is useful, briefly explains the category, and gives some examples of the ILE APIs available in that category.

Activation-Group and Control-Flow APIs

This set of APIs is useful for managing the activation group in which your programs execute. You have access to the call stack for registering and unregistering exit procedures, for controlling boundary information, and for registering exit routines for your activation groups. Some examples of these APIs are

- CEE4FCB: finds a control boundary
- CEE4RAGE: registers an exit routine for your activation group
- CEERTX: registers a call-stack entry termination user exit procedure
- CEEUTX: unregisters a call-stack entry termination user exit procedure

APIs for Managing Condition- or Exception-Handling

This set of bindable APIs lets you incorporate some of the specialized condition-handling techniques described in Chapter 9, "The Exception Model." Examples of these APIs are as follows.

- CEE4HC: handle a condition
- CEEMRCR: reposition the resume cursor to another point within the program receiving the exception message
- CEEHDLR: register a user-written condition handler
- CEEHDLU: unregister a user-written condition handler

Date- and Time-Manipulation APIs

This set of ILE APIs not only gives you the capability of obtaining the system date and time, but it also lets you set this information on the system. The following are just some of the APIs available in this category.

- CEEGMT: get Greenwich Mean Time
- CEEDATE: convert Julian date to character format
- CEEISEC: convert integers to seconds
- CEEDYWK: compute day-of-week from Julian date

Math APIs

The following are some of the APIs available in ILE for mathematical applications. (Note: the x in the API names indicates the data type of the result.)

- CEESxACS: compute arccosine
- CEESxATN: compute arctangent
- CEESxLG2: compute logarithm, base 2
- CEESxSQT: compute square root
- CEERANO: return a random number

Message-Handling APIs

These APIs let you get, format, and dispatch messages on the system.

- CEEMOUT: dispatch a message
- CEEMGET: get a message
- CEEMSG: get, format, and dispatch a message

Program- or Procedure-Call APIs

This set of specialized APIs deals with program and procedure calls. These APIs let you obtain information such as which arguments were omitted on the call to the program.

- CEETSTA: test for an omitted argument on the call to a procedure or program
- CEEDOD: retrieve operational descriptor information

Source-Debugger APIs

ILE lets HLLs access debug-related commands that otherwise would be available via the command line. The following are two examples of the APIs in this category.

- QteSubmitDebugCommand: lets a program issue debug statements
- QteStartSourceDebug: lets a session use the source debugger

Storage-Management APIs

The APIs in this category obtain and manipulate system heap space. The following are just few APIs in this category.

- CEECRHP: create heap
- CEEDSHP: discard heap
- CEERLHP: release heap

Note that these lists of APIs are not complete. See Appendix B for an exhaustive list of the available ILE APIs.

ILE's naming conventions for APIs are as follows: APIs that are consistent across all IBM SAA platforms have a name prefixed with the letters CEE. AS/400-specific APIs have names prefixed with the letters CEE4.

Conclusion

APIs provide a way to harness system-level function, and now you can bind the new APIs into your ILE programs. The range of functionality you can achieve through these APIs is broad and inestimably easier than trying to code the newly available functions yourself.

Some of the function APIs provide may be available at an HLL level. An example would be time functions. In ILE RPG, the TIME operation could be used to accomplish the same task as the API. On the other hand, there is much API function that is not available at the HLL level. For example, the CEExACS API provides the arccosine of a number. ILE RPG has no operation code that provides this function.

APIs are not the only system functions available to simplify your programming efforts and add functionality. One other area where the system helps you is in exception handling. OS/400 sends you messages when it encounters errors and can handle them for you. In ILE, you now also have the option of coding your own exception handlers. The next chapter explains the ILE exception-handling model, including your new options.

The Exception Model

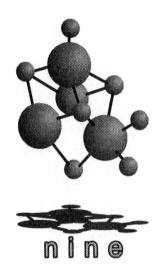

Generally, when the all-seeing operating system observes a program behaving in some way that the system deems unacceptable, it sends a message to call attention to the error. In ILE, we call these messages *exception messages*. A very common error for which the system generates an exception message is an *access violation*. An access violation occurs when an executing program is attempting to reach storage that is not within its allocated boundaries. Imagine, for example, a program that contains a pointer that is set to a list of items. In using the pointer to traverse the list, the programmer increments the pointer one too many times, thereby attempting to access an item that is beyond the boundaries of storage allocated for that list. When the program attempts to access this storage, the execution environment issues an exception message for the access violation.

Some systems may have different exception models from the one we just described. However, for ILE, the discussion that follows is based on this concept of exceptions as messages from the operating system.

What Is Exception Handling?

When we talk about *handling* exceptions, we're referring to the processing of an exception message during an application's runtime. Essentially, the system communicates exception situations by way of messages that pass through the various levels of the execution environment until the message is marked as processed, or *handled*. These various levels are represented by the program execution stack or *call stack*. (The call stack is a last-in, first-out structure that contains references to the active programs within an activation group.) Beginning with the stack entry in the top position on the execution stack, the message passes from entry to entry down through the execution stack until one entry marks it as handled. As a last resort, the system will finally handle any exception messages that are not handled otherwise.

When the system or the programmer sends an exception message, exception processing begins. That processing continues until that exception message is marked, or modified, in such a way that they system considers it *handled*.

Let us give an overview of what we mean by exception message processing. Processing begins when the system sends a message to the topmost entry in the call stack. For OPM, exception message processing calls handlers specific to OPM programs. Once the OPM exception message handler is called, the system modifies the exception message to indicate the handler has been called.

In the case of ILE, the particular HLL runtime will modify the exception message before calling any user-coded exception handler you may have provided. At this point, the HLL-specific error handling considers the exception message handled.

If HLL-specific error handling is not used, one of two things can occur.

1) The ILE HLL can either handle the exception message or

2) exception message processing will continue, and the system will send the message to the next-lower entry in the call stack. (Note that each ILE HLL may handle unhandled exception messages differently.) This type of exception message falls into the category of *unhandled exception default actions*.

The exception message is sent to each call stack entry in sequence until the message is modified, or marked as handled.

How Are Exception Messages Received?

Exception messages are received by means of a *call message queue* associated with each call stack entry. This message queue makes sending and receiving exception and informational messages among a particular call stack's entries possible. The call message queue for a particular call stack entry carries the same name as the ILE procedure or OPM program on the call stack. This is important because, through the use of APIs, you can send messages to a particular call stack entry. In case your call stack contains two entries for ILE procedures with the same name, you may also modify the module name and ILE program or service program name. Otherwise, the nearest call stack entry will receive the message queue.

Aside from the call message queues, each OS/400 job also is permitted one external message queue for all programs and procedures that are running within that job to use for sending and receiving messages between the interactive job and the user. To complement the ILE exception message model, user-accessible APIs are provided to all sending and receiving exception messages.

Who Sends Exception Messages?

OS/400, a message-handler API, HLL verbs, and an ILE API can all send exception messages. Let's look briefly at each of these possibilities.

System

OS/400 sends messages for the system or on behalf of an HLL to indicate a programming error or to provide status information.

Message-Handler API

You can use a message-handling API called QMHSNDPM to send an exception message to some particular call message queue.

Language-Specific Verbs

HLLs can give you specific functions or verbs to send exception messages.

ILE API

You can use the ILE API, CEESGL, to raise a condition in ILE that causes the system to send an escape exception message or status exception message.

What Kinds of Exception Messages Are There?

As we've said, ILE implements exceptions by way of exception messages. The message types that qualify as exception messages are escape, status, notify, and function-check messages.

Escape

*ESCAPE-type messages indicate that an error has occurred that will cause the executing program to end abnormally. The program will not receive control after an escape exception message.

Status

This type of message describes the status of work that a given program is doing. The manner in which the receiving program handles the incoming message determines whether the sender will receive control after having sent it.

Notify

*NOTIFY messages describe an execution condition requiring the user or program to respond or act. As with status messages, the manner in which the receiving program handles the incoming message determines whether the sender will receive control after having sent it.

Function Check

Function checks are essentially unexpected program behavior and mark the ending condition. ILE function checks are a special message type that only the system can send. OPM function checks carry the message identification of CPF9999.

Exception Message Percolation

ILE uses a process called *percolation* to handle conditions and exceptions. If a program, procedure, or function currently executing on a system declines to handle an exception message or condition, that exception or condition is passed to the next-lower entry in the call stack for handling. If, for example, the operating system generates an exception and passes it to the first entry on the stack, that procedure can handle it or pass it on to the next procedure. If that procedure doesn't handle the message either, it will pass to the next procedure. Of course, each procedure has the same option of handling the exception or passing it on.

This process of passing an exception down through the active call stack is known as *exception percolation*. Exception percolation continues down the stack until one entry handles this exception. If no entry handles it, the exception returns to the operating system.

After an exception message is received for a particular call-stack entry and before the message is percolated to the next call-stack entry, the following occurs: If a direct monitor is registered, the incoming exception message is handled. Otherwise, the system checks whether an ILE condition handler is registered. If so, the message is handled. If not, the system checks whether an HLL-specific handler can handle it. If yes, the message is handled. If not, the message is percolated.

To help you understand how all this talk about exception handling really works in ILE, let's look at Figure 9-1.

1. A runtime error has occurred in Procedure C. The system sends an exception message.

2. The top call-stack entry did not handle the exception message, so it is sent to the next-lower call-stack entry, Procedure B.

3. That entry does not handle the exception, so it is sent to the lowest call-stack entry, Procedure A.

4. No call-stack entry handles the exception message, sot it is passed to the operating system.

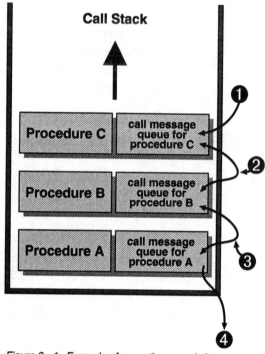

Figure 9 - 1: Example of exception percolation

Now that you have a general idea about percolation, let's look at how percolation happens in closer detail. A call-stack entry can be a user-written ILE procedure, program, or service program; a user-written OPM program; or a system program or procedure. Depending on the type of exception, the system gives the call-stack entry an opportunity to handle the exception via a user-written exception handler. (ILE supports two types of user-provided handlers, direct monitor handlers and ILE condition handler; we'll discuss these in detail in the next section.) If the application does not handle the exception, the system can pass it to the HLL's execution environment. The language environments may provide default handlers to process a certain set of exceptions that the programs written in those languages can generate. If still not handled, the exception is passed to the next entry on the call stack.

Certain exceptions can exist that the operating environment may classify as severe enough that no recovery is possible, so the operating system must handle them directly. An example of one such exception might be where the user program has caused a memory access violation. Usually, in such circumstances, the system cannot guarantee that the loaded program is still valid, so its execution should cease immediately. In such cases, percolation will not occur.

Types of Handlers

ILE enhances AS/400 exception management by providing various methods of handling exception messages. ILE's three layers of exception management are user-provided handlers, HLL-specific handlers, and the operating system. If you do not provide your own handler, the system resorts to the HLL-specific handler for the language in which the executing procedure (or OPM program) is written. As we described in our discussion of percolation, the operating system is the last resort. Let's look at each method in detail.

User-Provided Handlers

Like OS/2, ILE lets you handle exceptions within your HLL program. By coding your own exception handler, which you might call a message monitor, you can make your application more responsive to various situations. Consider an example of a program that assumes a particular data file exists in a particular library on the system. During execution, the program attempts to open that data file and receives an exception because the file does not exist. Rather than presenting the end user with an exception message, your program can intercept the exception and give the user the opportunity to indicate the library in which the file exists.

HLL-Specific Handlers

If you do not provide a user-written exception handler, the exception is passed to the second type of handlers, the HLL-specific handler. You do not register this type of handler. Rather, the ILE HLLs provide them. As their name suggests, these handlers are specific to the language that they support, so you need to refer to a particular language's documentation for details.

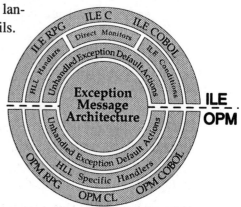

Nevertheless, as Figure 9-2 shows, there is consistency in what happens if a particular HLL-specific handler does not handle a given exception. This category of exceptions falls under the control of the unhandled exception action default for ILE. A separate unhandled exception action default is described for OPM.

Figure 9 - 2: ILE error-handling model

The Operating System

The last resort for unhandled exception messages is the operating system. The actions the system takes depend on the severity of the exception. As mentioned earlier, some exceptions are severe enough that the system will choose to terminate the entire application.

In OPM, if the associated exception handlers do not handle an exception, the system removes the entry, converts the message into a function check, and sends it to a previous call-stack entry. If the exception is never handled, the job ends. In ILE, the system gives each call stack a chance to handle the original message. Only then does the system convert the exception to a function check. At this point, the exception processing starts over, beginning with the caller of the procedure that incurred the exception. This time, the system gives each call stack entry a second chance to handle the function check. If the function check is not handled, the system sends a generic message, CEE9901. In our example, this message goes back to the RPG/400 OPM program.

Registering an Exception Handler

To let the system know that you want to use a particular user-written handler at runtime, you need to *register* that handler. Registering is simply the activity of making your user-coded handler known to the execution-time environment. (This capability should be familiar to OS/2 programmers who have used the DosSetExceptionHandler.) In ILE, to register an ILE procedure, you use the CEEHDLR API, which then receives control on the occurrence of an exception. When you want the high-level language or the system to handle exceptions again, you use the CEEHLDU bindable API to unregister a handler. You use the QMHCHGEM API to modify an exception message and mark it as handled.

Direct Monitors

There are two flavors of user-written handlers, *direct monitors* and ILE condition handlers. Direct monitors are user-provided exception handlers that are in effect for a specific program segment or block. That is, in ILE, you can have your exception handler actively monitor for exception messages during execution of the ILE procedure for a specific number of HLL statements. Note that this function may not be available in all ILE HLLs. In the ILE C, this function is available via the #pragme directive.

Condition Handlers

ILE condition handlers are more general than direct monitors. ILE lets you put a condition handler into effect at execution time, so that it remains active for a particular call stack entry. When activated, such handlers are said to be registered.

Condition Tokens

The ILE condition handler deals with the exception in the form of a *condition token*. Condition tokens are basically a mapping from the underlying exception message to some higher form that the HLL understands. It is this mapping from exception messages to conditions that results in the synonymous use of these two terms in the documentation. Condition tokens are an important concept because they free you from the detailed system implementation of the exception. A 12-byte data structure that is consistent across all SAA platforms represents conditions.

Note that ILE lets you register multiple condition handlers for a particular call stack entry. In the event of percolation, all registered condition handlers will be tried in a last-in, first-out manner, based on the order in which they were registered.

Resuming After an Exception

We've just seen that OS/400's ILE exception message architecture provides mapping between exceptions and conditions. And within this architecture, exceptions and conditions may interact. Consider an application
where you have registered your own condition handler by way of the
CEEHDLR bindable API. This condition handler then handles exception
messages sent via the QMHSNDPM API. (In the following discussion, the
term exception handler refers to both the OS/400 exception handler and
the ILE condition handler.)

Resume Point

After the system has sent an exception, you may want to resume execution of your program. This capability is especially useful in applications
that will tolerate certain kinds of errors or exceptions. For such situations, ILE has defined the concept of a *resume point*. Continuation after
an exception is possible from the resume point, which is initially set to
the program instruction immediately following the violating instruction.

Figure 9-3 illustrates the triggering of an exception and resumption of the program at the resume point.

```
/* Calculation program example....        */
...
read(x);                  /* if x = 0, then */
z = new_amount / x ; /* divide by zero */
                          /* exception will */
                          /* occur.         */
if x = 0 then
    while x = 0 do
        print("Divide by zero occurred, re-enter amount.");
        read(x) ;
        endwhile ;
endif;
...
```

Figure 9 - 3: Triggering an exception

In this example, if the program tolerates a divide-by-zero exception, the resume point would be the statement if x = 0 then. (Obviously, better programming practice would suggest that you move the test for x so that it is above the assignment of z, i.e., before the program executes the divide.)

Processing Exceptions with Handle and Resume Cursors

An understanding of how exceptions progress through the system and how you can control the point at which your program will resume execution after an exception has occurred depends on your understanding of the *handle cursor* and *resume cursor*. ILE uses the handle cursor to keep a pointer, or handle, on the current exception handler within the call stack at any moment during application execution. As an exception progresses through the system, ILE will search for the handler that is next in line within the call stack. In Figure 9-4, an exception occurs in procedure

C, and no handler within the handler list for the call-stack entry for procedure C handles the exception. As a result, the exception percolates to the previous call stack entry handler list, in this case, B. The handler to which the handle cursor first pointed would have been x1.x1, which did not handle the exception. Therefore, the handle cursor moved the handle to where it is presently pointing, x2.

The resume cursor is a pointer that maintains the current location, at which execution will continue once the exception has been handled. Generally, ILE will set the resume cursor to the first program instruction following the point at which the exception occurred. For previous call stack entries, the resume cursor is always the instruction following the point at which the program was suspended. Typically, as in the example above, programs are suspended because of a call that results in a new call-stack entry. In ILE, you can reset the resume cursor as you wish by way of the Move Resume Cursor (CEEMRCR) bindable API.

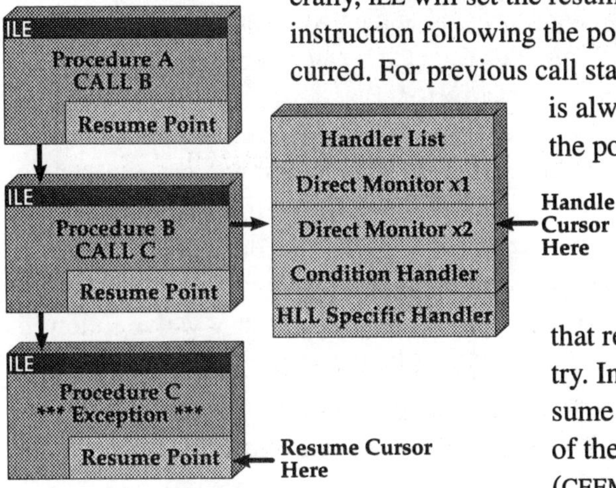

Figure 9-4: Resume and handle cursors

As we've seen, ILE can have many exception handlers within a call stack. These exception handlers are direct monitor handlers, ILE condition handlers, and HLL-specific handlers. In fact, not only can all three types of handlers exist within one call stack, but they may exist for one call stack entry, as in Figure 9-4.

Conclusion

OS/400, a message-handling API, HLL-specific verbs, and an ILE API can all send exception messages. These messages can be escape, status, notification, or function-check exception messages. The system percolates an exception message through the call stack, entry by entry, until the message is handled. User-provided handlers and HLL-specific handlers have an opportunity to handle an error, or the operating system can handle it. To inform the system that you want a user-written handler to handle an exception message, you register your handler. An additional function that the ILE exception model provides is that you can determine where you want processing to resume after an error.

As we've seen, ILE introduces several new models, functions, and tools, including the new exception model. A new tool that many programmers find one of the most interesting aspects of ILE is the debugging facility. Because the ILE debugger has several interesting new capabilities, the next chapter will depart a little from the overview format we've followed so far and actually show you how the debugger works.

Source-Level Debugging

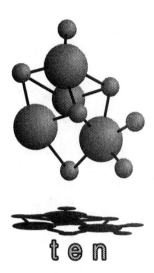

ILE's new debugger allows source-level debugging. This chapter will explain the debugger and show some details of how to use it. Up to now, this book has provided an overview of ILE and not attempted to demonstrate how to use its capabilities. This chapter departs a bit from that pattern and shows a little about how the ILE debugger works. We want to provide some examples so you'll get a feeling for this new tool.

ten

What Can the New Debugger Do?

The source-level debugger can debug ILE programs and service programs. In addition, the debugger can debug up to 10 OPM programs at one time. The facility has the intelligence to determine whether you created a program in ILE or in OPM. To start the debugger for both types of programs, you execute the same command, STRDBG (Start Debug).

You can use this debugger with a source file. You can set breakpoints by simply moving the cursor to the line where you want the breakpoint and then pressing a function key. In addition, you can display variables and step into or over an instruction. You can do all this without ever having to enter a command on the command line, but the debugger also introduces several useful new commands that you can execute when you need them.

In our overview of the various functions the ILE debugger provides, we will use an ILE C/400 program as an example. However, you can use the same function of the debugger with any ILE language.

Creating a Source Program

The simple C program we will use (we're calling it HELLO and putting it in library FARR) declares two fields as integers. Next, it performs a multiplication, and finally it prints the result. This simple program may have no real use, but it does illustrate the debugger's capabilities. As we will later see, the example program includes variables and an assignment statement so we can demonstrate how to place breakpoints at different statements and also how to display and change the values of variables.

Once we've coded a source member, we compile it as a *MODULE and create the program by executing CRTPGM. In the CRTCMOD command, we specify *PRINT on the OUTPUT parameter to cause the compiler to produce a source listing. Also, we specify the *ALL option on the DBGVIEW parameter, which tells the compiler that we need it to produce all debug tables. For the DBGVIEW parameter, we may choose one of five options: *NONE, *ALL, *STMT, *SOURCE, or *LIST. The default is *NONE, which disables all the debug options for debugging the compiled module object. We use this option when doing the final compile on our production programs. The *ALL option, which we used to debug the sample C program, enables all the debug options for the compiled module object and produces a source view, as well as a listing view. *STMT lets us debug the compiled module object, using program statement numbers and symbolic identifiers. *SOURCE generates the source view for debugging the compiled module object. Finally, *LIST generates the listing view for debugging the compiled module object. After executing CRTPGM, we can start a debug session.

Starting and Conducting a Source-Debug Session

Because we used the *ALL option on the DBGVIEW parameter, the program we are about to debug contains all the debugging views. To start a debug session for the HELLO program we created, we issue the following STRDBG command.

```
STRDBG   PGM(FARR/HELLO)
```

Figure 10-1 is the screen that is displayed as a result of starting the debug session (which remains active until we enter the ENDDBG (End Debug) command). This display shows the source of the main program we wrote in ILE C.

```
                         Display Module Source
Program:  HELLO            Library:  FARR         Module:  HELLO
    1
    2   #define interest 10
    3   #include <stdio.h>
    4   #include <ctype.h>
    5
    6   int main(void)
    7   {
    8      int amount=200;
    9      int result;
   10
   11
   12      result=amount*interest;
   13      printf ("The result is --->%d",result);
   14   }
                                                            Bottom
Debug . . .
F3=End program F6=Add/Clear breakpoint F10=Step F11=Display variable
F12=Resume     F13=Work with module breakpoints F24=More keys
```

Figure 10 - 1: Starting a debug session

Note that on the STRDBG command, we do not have to specify what kind of program we are about to debug. Is it an ILE program or is it an OPM program? The debugger has the intelligence to determine the various program types. In fact, we could mix OPM and ILE programs in the same debugging session, and the debugger would know how to treat each kind of program.

The debug screen displays the DEBUG command line where we may enter the various debug commands, such as ADDPGM (Add Program) or RMVPGM (Remove Program). In addition, at the bottom of the screen, we have a choice of many predefined function keys for use in a debug session.

Setting and Removing Breakpoints

Debugging a program basically involves two activities: 1) setting breakpoints to check for certain values and 2) running the program to observe its behavior. The new debugger makes these activities easy.

As you debug your program, you may want to stop at a certain statement to display or change the value of a variable. To do so, you set conditional and unconditional breakpoints. A conditional breakpoint stops the program when a specific condition at a specific statement is true. For example, you may want to stop at a statement when the content of field A equals 100. In contrast, an unconditional statement stops at a breakpoint or statement every time the statement is encountered.

The two ways to set unconditional and conditional breakpoints are by pressing F6 (Add/Clear breakpoints) or by pressing F13 (Work with breakpoints). To add a breakpoint, move the cursor to the statement where you want a breakpoint added, and press F6. Figure 10-2 is an example of setting a breakpoint at statement number 12. As the figure shows, this statement will be highlighted, and a message will appear at the bottom of the screen.

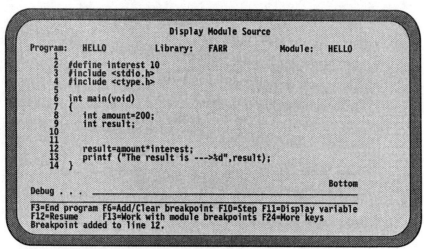

```
                        Display Module Source
Program:   HELLO          Library:   FARR        Module:   HELLO
     1
     2     #define interest 10
     3     #include <stdio.h>
     4     #include <ctype.h>
     5
     6     int main(void)
     7     {
     8          int amount=200;
     9          int result;
    10
    11
    12          result=amount*interest;
    13          printf ("The result is --->%d",result);
    14     }

                                                             Bottom
Debug . . . _____

F3=End program F6=Add/Clear breakpoint F10=Step F11=Display variable
F12=Resume     F13=Work with module breakpoints F24=More keys
Breakpoint added to line 12.
```

Figure 10 - 2: Adding breakpoint at statement number 12

To view the various breakpoints you set in your program, press F13. Figure 10-3 is the screen that you will see. This screen shows how you can set a conditional breakpoint. For example, you can set a condition such as "result=2000" to force the program to stop at statement 13 if that value occurs there.

```
                       Work with Module Breakpoints
                                                    System: AS400A
    Program . . . :   HELLO              Library . . . :  FARR
      Module . . . :   HELLO              Type . . . . . :  *PGM

    Type options, press Enter.
      1=Add   4=Clear

    Opt   Line      Condition
      1     13        result=2000
      _     12




    Command
    ===>
    F3=Exit   F4=Prompt   F5=Refresh   F9=Retrieve   F12=Cancel
```

Figure 10 - 3: Adding a condition at statement number 13

When you press the Enter key, the debugger adds the breakpoint and the condition to the table. When you are finished with this screen, press Enter or F12 to return. When you are finished adding breakpoints, you leave the debugger by pressing F3. Don't worry — all your breakpoints are saved.

Running the Program

You have set two breakpoints in your program, one unconditional at statement 12 and one conditional at statement 13. To try them out, run the program by executing the following command.

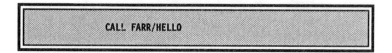

```
    CALL FARR/HELLO
```

When statement 12 is reached, the program stops. The Display Module Source display appears again, as in Figure 10-4.

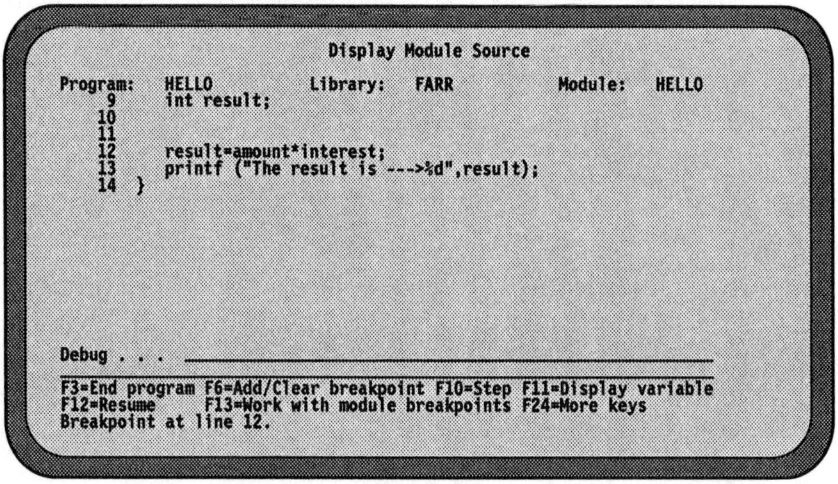

```
                        Display Module Source
Program:   HELLO          Library:   FARR        Module:   HELLO
    9      int result;
   10
   11
   12      result=amount*interest;
   13      printf ("The result is --->%d",result);
   14  }




Debug . . .  _____

F3=End program F6=Add/Clear breakpoint F10=Step F11=Display variable
F12=Resume      F13=Work with module breakpoints F24=More keys
Breakpoint at line 12.
```

Figure 10 - 4: Running the program with breakpoints

At this point, the debugger highlights statement 12 and waits for you to enter a command. If you want to see the value of a field, move the cursor to that field and press F11. For example, to see the value of field amount, move the cursor anywhere under field amount and press F11. Figure 10-5 is the screen that will appear.

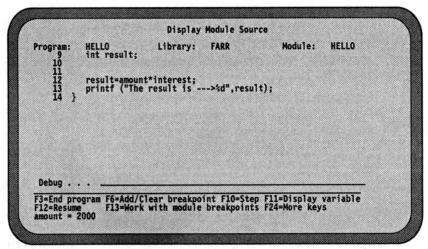

Figure 10 - 5: Displaying a value of a field

The source debugger displays the value of amount at the bottom of the screen.

To resume executing your program, press F12. Because we added a conditional breakpoint when result=2000, the debugger will check the value of result at this breakpoint to see if it is 2000. In this case, since result *is* 2000, the debugger will stop and inform you of this fact. Figure 10-6 is the screen that will appear.

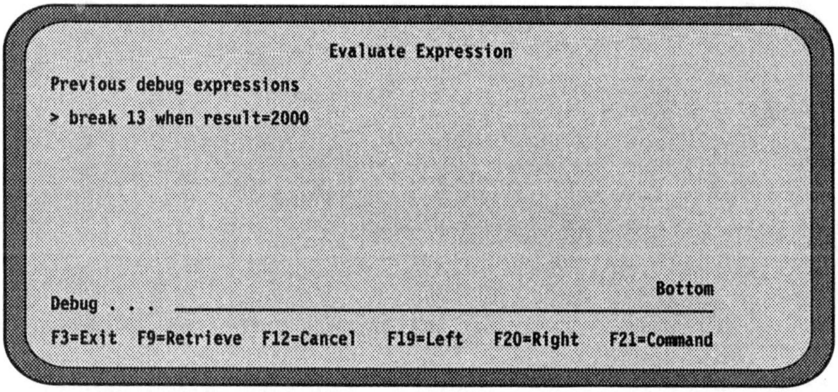

Figure 10 - 6: Stopping at a condition

Notice the options available at the bottom of this screen. The main one to note is F21, which lets you open a window and execute an OS/400 command. Figure 10-7 shows the screen that appears when you press function key 21.

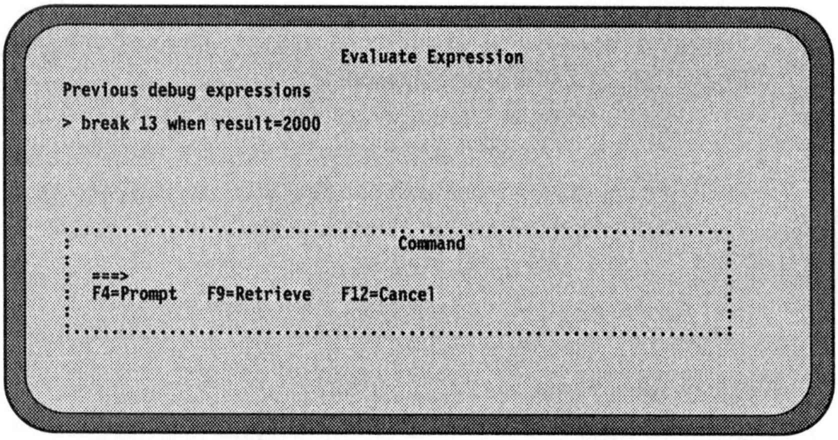

Figure 10 - 7: Command window

When you are finished with this screen, press F3. Also, press F12 to resume the execution of your program. When your program ends, the debugger returns you to the command line.

Debug Commands

Since we've landed at the command line, let's stop for a while and see what kinds of new debugger commands are available if you need to enter them here. As we mentioned, you don't ever *have* to enter commands to use the ILE source-level debugger, but you might want to take advantage of some of the powerful capabilities of the commands developed just for debugging. In this section, we will describe commands that may come in handy in your debug session.

How to Enter Debug Commands

Entering debug commands from the command line is straightforward and almost foolproof because you can enter a command in just about any form, and the debugger will probably recognize it. These commands are designed so that you can enter them in uppercase, lowercase, or mixed case. You can even abbreviate a command to the smallest subset of letters that uniquely identifies it. So, for example, for the `eval` command (which we'll explain in detail in the next section), you can type EVAL, eval, Eval, or even EVL on the command line.

Debug Command Descriptions

The available debug commands are `equate`, `display`, `break`, `clear`, `qual`, and `step`. Let's look at each command and how to use it.

`Equate`: The `equate` command lets you assign an expression, variable, or debug command to a name for shorthand use. The name must be a character string with no blanks. The definition must be a character string separated from the name by at least one blank. For example,

```
equate field1  amount*2-1000/300
```

You can now use field1 in debug commands in place of the string amount*2-1000/300

Display: The display command lets you display the names and definitions you've assigned by using the equate command. It also lets you display a different source module from the one currently shown on the Display Module Source display.

Break: The break command lets you enter either an unconditional or a conditional breakpoint at a position in the program you are testing. The position can be one of the following.

- Line_number: A line number of the source file for the module.

- Procedure_name/statement_number: The name of a procedure contained in the module, followed by a slash, followed by a statement number in the procedure.

You can use the break command or F6 (Add/Clear breakpoint) to enter an unconditional breakpoint. An unconditional breakpoint causes the program to stop just before the position entered.

You enter a conditional breakpoint by typing the break command, followed by the statement number, followed by the expression. The expression must have a Boolean or logical value. The expression is evaluated just before the statement runs that is at the position entered. If the value of the expression is true, or if there is an error evaluating the expression, the program stops and the Display Module Source display appears. If the value is false, the program does not stop.

Clear: The clear command removes conditional and unconditional breakpoints. If you specify a position, the clear command removes the breakpoint at that position. The position can be a line number or procedure name/statement number.

- Line_number: A line number of the source file for the module.

- Procedure_name/statement_number: The name of a procedure contained in the module, followed by a slash, followed by a statement number in the procedure.

If you specify the reserved word "PGM", clear removes all breakpoints in the program that contains the module being displayed.

Qual: The qual command lets you define the scope of variables that appear in subsequent eval commands, based on the position you specify on the qual command. The position can be either a line number or a procedure name/statement number.

- Line_number: A line number of the source file for the module (as shown on the Display Module Source display).

- Procedure_name/statement_number: The name of a procedure contained in the module, followed by a slash, followed by a statement number in the procedure (as shown on a listing of the program.)

Step: The step command lets you run one or more statements of the program you are debugging. To indicate the number of statements to run, you use the statement "count" (which must be a positive integer) in the step command. The program begins on the next statement.

If the reserved word "over" appears in a step command, procedure and function calls count as single statements. If the reserved word "into" appears in a step command, each statement in a procedure or function called counts as a step. "Over" is the default.

Only procedures and modules that contain debug data can be stepped into. Other programs cannot be stepped into.

Using the Eval Command to Change a Variable

To illustrate the use of the debug commands, let's look at some ways to use eval. We can issue an eval command on the debug command line when the program stops running at a breakpoint. The eval command lets us display and evaluate the value of expressions, arrays, or records or display or change the value of a field or variable. For example, in Figure 10-8, we issue the command eval amount*2-1000/300 to evaluate an expression.

```
                        Display Module Source
Program:  HELLO          Library:  FARR          Module:  HELLO
   10
   11
   12      result=amount*interest;
   13      printf ("The result is --->%d",result);
   14  }



                                                    Bottom
Debug . . .    eval amount*2-1000/300

F3=End program F6=Add/Clear breakpoint F10=Step F11=Display variable
F12=Resume     F13=Work with module breakpoints F24=More keys
Breakpoint at line 13.
```

Figure 10 - 8: Using eval command

According to the rules, amount is first multiplied by 2. This results in the value 400. Next, 1000 is divided by 300, and then it is subtracted from 400.

The result, 397, is then displayed at the bottom of the screen as shown in Figure 10-9.

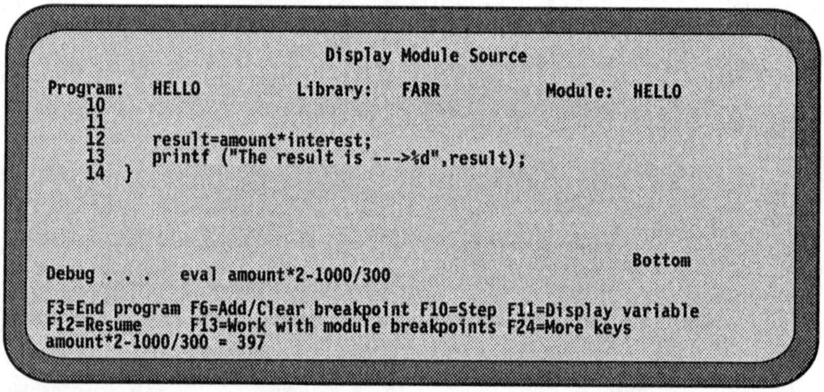

```
                         Display Module Source
Program:     HELLO          Library:    FARR          Module:   HELLO
    10
    11
    12        result=amount*interest;
    13        printf ("The result is --->%d",result);
    14  }



Debug . . .    eval amount*2-1000/300                             Bottom

F3=End program F6=Add/Clear breakpoint F10=Step F11=Display variable
F12=Resume     F13=Work with module breakpoints F24=More keys
amount*2-1000/300 = 397
```

Figure 10 - 9: Display of result of eval command

As another example, we can use an eval command to change the value of a field or variable by specifying "=" in an expression. The expression to the right of the equals sign is evaluated and assigned to the field or variable. When the debugger stops at the breakpoint on line 13, we enter the eval expression with an equals sign and a value on the right of the equals sign, as illustrated in Figure 10-10.

```
                           Display Module Source
Program:   HELLO           Library:   FARR          Module:  HELLO
     10
     11
     12     result=amount*interest;
--->13     printf ("The result is --->%d",result);
     14  }




                                                              Bottom
Debug . . .   eval result=9999

F3=End program F6=Add/Clear breakpoint F10=Step F11=Display variable
F12=Resume     F13=Work with module breakpoints F24=More keys
Breakpoint at line 13.
```

Figure 10 - 10: Changing the value of a variable

As we said, when we use the equals sign in an eval command, this statement acts as an assignment statement, assigning to the field or variable
any value we specify on the right of the equals sign. If we want the field
or variable in this example to be assigned the value 9999, we enter 9999 to
the right of the equals sign, as in Figure 10-10. As a result, this field or
variable now has the value 9999.

As we've seen, although we can debug programs without ever issuing a
debug command, the debug commands can be very helpful. They are a
tool that ILE provides to make debugging flexible and easy.

Helpful Debugging Displays

Before we finish this chapter, we should take note of some additional
tools for debugging. These tools are the Work with Module List display
and the Display Module Source: Select View display.

Work with Module List

To access the Work with Module List display, press Function key 14. From this display we can add programs to debug, remove programs, and work with specific module breakpoints.

Selecting Different Views

Since we compiled our sample programs with the DBGVIEW(*ALL), the debug information available to the program contains all views. To select a view, we can press function key 15 to get the Display Module Source: Select View display. This panel tells what the current view is and gives options for alternative views.

Conclusion

ILE's source-level debugger is a flexible tool that lets you perform debugging tasks without issuing any commands. However, if you need commands, new ones are available, and they provide additional function. And this tool is not limited to ILE programs. You can use it to debug OPM programs as well as ILE programs.

The ten chapters up to now have covered the basics of ILE and discussed the ILE APIs, the exception-handling model, and the new source-level debugger. This overview is meant to give you an idea of what ILE is all about. But because this is just an overview, if you're like most people we've talked to about ILE, you still have some questions. That's why we've included the following chapter. It covers the questions people ask us most frequently and then gives you our answers.

Frequently Asked Questions

We hope we have answered many of your questions about ILE. However, in the event that we haven't, we'd like to discuss some of the questions we receive most frequently during presentations and discussions. Although we have grouped the questions by topic, you will discover that many topics really overlap. After you've read this section, if some aspects of the material in this book are still unclear, we will be happy to answer any further questions you would like to send to us in care of CAS.

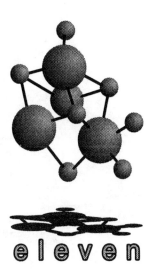

eleven

Service Programs

Q What restrictions apply to service programs that may or may not apply to other objects of the type *PGM?

A Compared to other *PGM-type objects, service programs impose two restrictions: First, you must have *CHANGE authority for the library where you are creating the service program, and second, you must have *USE authority to the specified modules, service programs, and binding directories. These restrictions have much to do with the fact that service programs are not callable programs. Rather, they are building blocks to create applications.

Q How do I create a service program?

A You specify a set of modules and/or binding directories on the CRTSRVPGM (Create Service Program) command and execute it to create a bound service program. Figure 11-1 shows the parameters available on the CRTSRVPGM command. As with most CL commands, CRTSRVPGM, supports prompting.

```
                    Create Service Program (CRTSRVPGM)

 Type choices, press Enter.

 Service program . . . . . . . .   Arith         Name
   Library . . . . . . . . . . .     TOPIWALA    Name, *CURLIB
 Module . . . . . . . . . . . .    *SRVPGM       Name, generic*, *SRVPGM
   Library . . . . . . . . . . .                 Name, *LIBL, *CURLIB...
                   + for more values

 Export . . . . . . . . . . . .   *SRCFILE       *SRCFILE, *ALL
 Export source file . . . . . . .  QSRVSRC       Name, QSRVSRC
   Library . . . . . . . . . . .     *LIBL       Name, *LIBL, *CURLIB
 Export source member . . . . . .  *SRVPGM       Name, *SRVPGM
 Text 'description' . . . . . . .  *BLANK
                          Additional Parameters

 Bind service program . . . . . .  *NONE         Name, generic*, *NONE,
   Library . . . . . . . . . . .                 Name, *LIBL
                   + for more values

 Binding directory . . . . . . .   *NONE         Name, *NONE
   Library . . . . . . . . . . .                 Name, *LIBL, *CURLIB...
                   + for more values

 Activation group . . . . . . . .  *CALLER       Name, *CALLER
 Creation options . . . . . . . .                *GEN, *NOGEN, *NODUPPR
                   + for more values
 Listing detail . . . . . . . . .  *NONE         *NONE, *BASIC, *EXTEND
 User profile . . . . . . . . . .  *USER         *USER, *OWNER
 Replace program . . . . . . . .   *YES          *YES, *NO
 Authority . . . . . . . . . . .   *LIBCRTAUT    Name, *LIBCRTAUT, *CHANGE
```

Figure 11 - 1: CRTSRVPGM Command

A few parameters on this command may not be familiar to AS/400 programmers. Let's look at some of them in the order in which they appear on the screen.

Service program specifies the name of the service program you're creating.

Library specifies the name of the library where you want to create the service program.

Module lists the names of the modules to be bound by copy to create the service program object. If the system finds duplicate module and library specifications, it uses only the first instance of the duplicate module and library. Then the system copies modules in this list into the final service program object. The *SRVPGM parameter lets you specify a service program as part of this service program.

Export specifies the names of the data items and procedures this service program exports (makes externally available). That is, it gives the names that bound programs and service programs may import. The SRCFILE parameter lets you specify a member of a source file.

Bind service program specifies the service programs that may have exports that will be needed during the binder phase of program creation. If one of these service programs does provide an export, the name of the service program and the library specified are saved with the created bound program or service program. When this newly created program or service program is activated, the service programs that were found to be needed (because they provided an export) are searched for and also activated. (The system activates a service program from this list only when this program or service program is activated.) The search criteria are determined by the library specification or the command. If a library was specified, the system searches that library for the service program to be activated. If *LIBL was specified, the library list is searched.

Q How many service programs can I call from a program?

A You don't call service programs. As with DLLs in OS/2, OS/400 exposes entry points so that programs that have service programs bound to them can call those entry points. Because entry points are usually procedures (or functions, as with ILE C), you call procedures and refer to data items whose names have been exported by those service programs. You can bind to a maximum of about 32,000 service programs from one program or service program.

Q What kind of overhead is associated with using multiple service programs?

A Dividing an application into multiple service programs will mainly affect application startup, that is, program activation. Most of the impact is in resolving pointers to the service programs and building the linking structures required during the execution of the application in question.

For most applications, this impact will be extremely small when compared to overall application runtime. ILE designers have focused on minimizing program activation time and establishing the required program linkages. When compared to an equivalent OPM- or EPM-based application, ILE program startup is much faster.

Q Can one service program call another service program?

A Yes, one service program can call a procedure within another service program. It is important to keep in mind that you are not calling the service program. Rather, you are calling some procedure within that service program. And, of course, that procedure's name must be defined as an exported item.

Q How large should a service program be? How many modules should I have in my service program?

A This question has no direct answer. However, when you're looking at this issue, you should consider development and maintenance, packaging, and performance.

1. *Development and Maintenance*: One philosophy would dictate that we design service programs to be tight in function, grouping only adjacent functions and exporting only a few entry points from those service programs. The reasoning behind this methodology would be that any change to underlying function (i.e., building block or support function that reusable service programs provide) should not affect the application components that use the service programs. Consider the following example.

A pizza franchise updates customer information on every order, adding information such as size of pizza ordered, ingredients, and drinks ordered. Now, assume that the database that retains this information is at a central site, and each franchise location has the hardware and software to connect with the central site to make those customer updates. Assume that the software that provides the connection to the central site is a service program. We will refer to this software as *connection support*. If the MIS department decides to rewrite connection support to use TCP/IP rather than standard workstation support, it would be important to keep the impact on the entire application as small as possible. The impact depends greatly on the application design and, more specifically, on the connection-support component.

If the connection support service program contains the minimum code for the communications only, the enhancement should not affect other portions of the application installation. However, had MIS designed connection support to include local database retrieval and perhaps the central-site posting-request software, other areas of the application would also, unnecessarily, be affected.

In this example, it makes sense to keep the function that a service program provides minimal and tight. MIS can rewrite and recompile connection support and rebind it into the application installation without much concern for irrelevant application dependencies.

Going overboard in practicing such methodology, however, has its down side: Application startup time will degrade if the application has a large number of these small service programs. It is your responsibility to weigh relevant factors.

2. *Packaging*: You can use service programs to implement an API. To address situations where program use of an API should not be exposed beyond the service program that requires it, you can use service programs. If such API access is important to the application developer, this can result in service programs whose sole purpose is to hide the API, thereby adding to total number of service programs in the application.

As Figure 11-2 illustrates, the service program PROG_0 does not export the procedure that makes the API call. By not exporting this procedure, you can hide the API call.

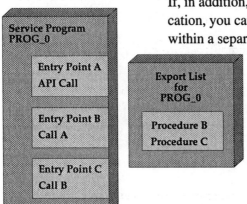

Figure 11 - 2: Hiding API calls

If, in addition, you require protection from the application, you can execute the service program from within a separate activation group. Because each activation group can maintain its own addressable storage, stack, and heap management, this approach will shield your application from errors that may make recovery impossible. You should realize, however, that bound calls to programs executing in separate activation groups are approximately twice as slow as bound calls to programs that will execute within the same activation group.

3. *Performance*: You may wish to minimize the number of service programs that are used, and therefore loaded, during program activation and wish to maintain larger, more general service programs to create the application. Applications using service programs pay a performance price. Whenever such applications reference any object that the current service program exports, the system must resolve a system pointer to obtain a handle to that object. If an application uses service programs that themselves contain inter-service-program references, this penalty may become noticeable.

You should strive for a design that will package service programs in a way that minimizes the number of inter-service-program references. This packaging will, in turn, reduce the amount of system pointer resolution during execution and greatly reduce the amount of time required to build the inter-service-program linkage information.

Static area allocation and initialization is another cost associated with service programs. When you combine multiple modules into a service program, the system allocates and initializes a single static area for the service program, thereby reducing this cost.

As a final point, your service program design should attempt to group frequently used function. This will minimize the size of your service programs.

Q Can you send service programs to an AS/400 that does not have an ILE compiler?

A Yes. Service programs will run on any AS/400 that has OS/400 V2R3 or later, providing that the ILE version of the language you used to develop that service program is available on that release of OS/400.

Debug Support

Q Does the new source debugger replace the old debugger? Will the old debugger work with ILE programs?

A No. The new ILE source debugger supports only ILE programs. IBM will continue to support the existing debugger for debugging programs you've generated with a non-ILE compiler. The STRDBG command starts all debug support for OPM as well as ILE programs. The existing debugger must remain to support the OPM languages, and the ILE debugger has been designed to co-exist in the same debug session with that debugger. However, the ILE debugger does not support existing debugger line commands, such as DSPPGMVAR and ADDBKP. The advantage, however, will be that the debugger for ILE languages will be much more versatile, usable, and richer in function than the existing debugger. Some of the ILE source-level debugger features let you

- debug at the listing, source, or statement level
- point and shoot to examine the contents of a variable
- point to set and remove breakpoints
- evaluate an expression using the debugger EVAL line command

Q

Do you need to compile differently to use the debugger?

A

The CRTxxxMOD and the CRTBNDxxx commands have debug options available for all ILE compilers. These commands let you control the debugging views to be included with your compiled program object. The debugging view essentially dictates the source level you want to include with the compiled program object. For example, *STMT indicates that source will show on the debug screen and will include program statement numbers and symbols. RPG programmers may understand this point in terms of the view that contains the COPY members expanded, as opposed to a view where the COPY members are not expanded. The *STMT debugging view does not include COPY members, whereas the *LIST debug view does. C programmers can relate this to the *LIST view, where macros are expanded, as opposed to the *STMT view, where they are not.

The default for debugging views is *NONE: The system produces no debugging tables, and therefore, the program cannot execute in debug mode. Figure 11-3 shows the debugging view parameter on the CRTxxxMOD and the CRTBNDxxx commands.

```
Debugging view . . . . . .  *NONE          *NONE, *ALL, *LIST...
```

Figure 11 - 3: Parameter to specify debugging view

If you want to run your program under debug, you must spec-
ify one of the following values on the create command:
*NONE, *ALL, *SOURCE, *LIST. See Chapter 10 for details about
ILE's source-level debugger.

ILE Languages

Q   Will ILE mark the end of the existing OPM compilers?

A   It is the end for EPM C/400, System C/400, and APTA (Application Performance Tuning Aid; this tool helps you get better
performance with C applications). IBM continues to support
the OPM RPG and COBOL compilers. However, IBM is planning
future enhancements only for the ILE compilers, rather than
OPM RPG and COBOL.

Q   Why is C/400 the first ILE language available in V2R3?

A   As discussed earlier, many of C/400's performance problems
are due to overhead associated with the EPM model. To improve C/400's viability as a development language, IBM found
it important to resolve such performance problems as soon as
possible. The new ILE model will provide benefits to all ILE
languages, but in terms of performance, C/400 will benefit the
most. In addition, since IBM's developers used ILE C/400 to

write the ILE RPG and ILE COBOL compilers, they first had to develop ILE C as an enabling technology.

Q What is the performance improvement for C programs?

A The range of performance benefit will be wide for C programs migrating to ILE C. Benchmarks indicate performance is 1.5 to 2 times better from code optimization alone. These benchmarks tested loop-intensive code segments with heavy array use. You can expect that I/O-intensive programs will also experience performance gains from ILE, but they will not be as great.

Q What is the performance gain in static calls compared to the dynamic call we use today?

A The system performs all static resolution at program creation time, in contrast with dynamic calls, for which resolution occurs at runtime. As a result, static calls perform much faster than dynamic calls. A bound call to a function with one parameter within the same activation group is approximately 5 times faster than an unbound call to the same function in EPM. The estimate for bound calls into another activation group is that they are 3 times faster than unbound calls. This comparison refers specifically to EPM and ILE. You can expect further gains for OPM and ILE application comparisons.

Q Are dynamic calls still allowed in RPG?

A Yes, RPG continues to support dynamic calls by means of the CALL operation code, however, you can dynamically call only programs (objects with the *PGM attribute). For static calls, you use the newly introduced CALLB (Call Bound) operation code.

Q   Is a migration aid packaged with the compilers?

A   For ILE C/400, the migration aid (CVTCSRC) is in the QUSRTOOLS library. This utility will let you investigate the ease of moving to ILE before buying the compiler. Early customer tests indicate that more than 90 percent of programs did not require any conversion. The RPG migration utility (CVTRPGPGM) to convert OPM RPG source to ILE RPG format will be shipped with the compiler.

Performance

Q   Is there a performance penalty for creating programs with debug information?

A   No penalty should result from executing code created with debug information. However, if the question concerns compile-time performance, the answer is yes. The compiler must generate certain extra program information to debug-enable that program. For example, the compiler has to generate type tables to tell the debugger the types (e.g., character, zoned, packed) of the fields in the program. Another example is LOC statements to indicate line numbers for breakpoints.

You should not specify optimization if you intend to debug the module. You should generate optimized code as a final compiler option before your application goes to production.

Q Do you have to bind all possible programs that could be called? Can you call with a variable name?

A Binding of constituent modules occurs automatically when you issue CRTPGM to compile all ILE programs. Binding also occurs when you issue CRTSRVPGM to compile service programs. Programs using service programs bind to those service programs. Thus, for inter-service-program calls, where one service program refers to the exported procedure of another, those calls are bound (i.e., you must use the CALLB operation).

However, no binding is necessary if your program is issuing only dynamic calls to ILE or OPM programs. For example, if your ILE program calls an OPM program, no binding is involved, and you use the CALL operation.

As for variable names, yes. You can call with a variable name by way of COBOL's *CALL identifier* or the RPG *CALL op-code*; but the system assumes the target is a program rather than a procedure unless the target exists in the same module, which can be true only for nested COBOL (ANSI 85 high) programs.

RPG supports calling procedures by variable name, pointer, literal, or named constant. You must bind into the application all programs that are referenced by any CALLB operation codes in the program, and of course, those programs can be service programs or other modules.

Q Can I expect a utility to help me find all called program or procedure names?

A No such utility is planned for the first release of ILE.

Commands

Q   How is the CRTPGM command different from its OPM equivalent?

A   The best way to give a detailed answer to this question is to show you the parameters of CRTPGM. Figure 11-4 shows the parameters.

```
                    Create Program (CRTPGM)
 Type choices, press Enter.

 Program . . . . . . . . . . . . .   X           Name
   Library . . . . . . . . . . .     *CURLIB     Name, *CURLIB
 Module . . . . . . . . . . . . .    *PGM        Name, generic*, *PGM, *
   Library . . . . . . . . . . .                 Name, *LIBL, *CURLIB...
             + for more values

 Text 'description' . . . . . . .    *ENTMODTXT

                    Additional Parameters

 Program entry procedure module      *ONLY       Name, *ONLY, *FIRST
   Library . . . . . . . . . . .                 Name, *LIBL, *CURLIB...
 Bind service program . . . . . .    *NONE       Name, generic*, *NONE,
   Library . . . . . . . . . . .                 Name, *LIBL
             + for more values

 Binding directory . . . . . . .     *NONE       Name, *NONE
   Library . . . . . . . . . . .                 Name, *LIBL, *CURLIB...
             + for more values

 Activation group . . . . . . . .    *NEW        Name, *NEW, *CALLER
 Creation options . . . . . . . .                *GEN, *NOGEN, *NODUPPRO
             + for more values
 Listing detail . . . . . . . . .    *NONE       *NONE, *BASIC, *EXTENDE
 User profile . . . . . . . . . .    *USER       *USER, *OWNER
 Replace program . . . . . . . .     *YES        *YES, *NO
 Authority . . . . . . . . . . .     *LIBCRTAUT  Name, *LIBCRTAUT, *CHAN
```

Figure 11 - 4: Create program command

You can display this panel on your AS/400 by typing CRTPGM and PF4. Let's examine a few of the command's parameters as they appear on the screen shown in Figure 11-4.

Program entry procedure module: This parameter specifies the name of the module that will contain the program entry procedure specification for this program — that is, the name of the procedure that the system will call upon application startup. Possible values for this parameter are *ONLY, *FIRST, or a name.

ONLY: Of all the modules to be bound by copy to create this program object, only one module may have a procedure identified as the program entry procedure. With *ONLY, you aren't specifying a module. You are specifying that, of the modules to be bound by copy (either from the MODULE parameter or the binding directory), only one can have a PEP.

FIRST: The system will select as the program entry procedure the first module in the list of modules to have a program entry procedure specification.

Name: The system will select the module named here as the program entry procedure. The named module must contain a procedure identified as the PEP. An error can result if the module does not contain a PEP.

Binding directory (BNDDIR): This parameter specifies the name of the binding directory that contains a list of modules and service programs that the system will use in external symbol resolution. (Symbol resolution is the process of resolving the names of imported procedures and data items with the names of exported procedures and data items.)

Activation group (ACTGRP): This parameter specifies the activation group this program is associated with when called. The possible values for this parameter are *NEW, *CALLER, and Activation-group-name.

NEW: Calling this program creates a new activation group. This called program is then associated with the newly created activation group.

CALLER: When this program is called, it is executed in the caller's activation group.

Activation-group-name: Specify the name of the particular activation group to be used when the program is called.

Q

CRTPGM doesn't specify a language. What attribute will the system display when you execute a DSPOBJD command on this program?

A

The system propagates the attribute of the module that contained the program entry procedure, and this becomes the attribute for the created ILE program.

Q

What does DSPPGMREF (Display Program Reference) show?

A

DSPPGMREF shows the ILE service programs that are needed. To see the list of modules that were used to create the ILE program, specify DSPPGM. DSPPGM support is enhanced to display this information for ILE programs. The behavior of DSPPGM for existing programs will remain unaffected.

Q Will I be able to use DSPMOD (Display Module) to examine a
module's attributes?

A Yes. Figure 11-5 shows the information you can expect to see
when using the DSPMOD command.

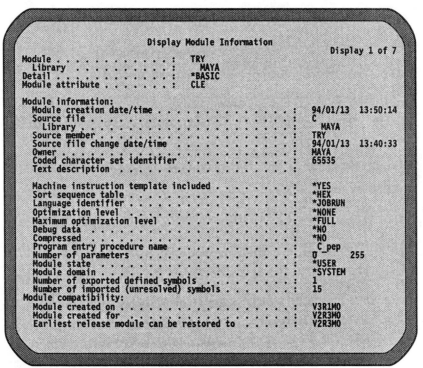

```
                    Display Module Information
                                                   Display 1 of 7
Module . . . . . . . . . . . . :    TRY
   Library . . . . . . . . . . :       MAYA
Detail . . . . . . . . . . . . :    *BASIC
Module attribute . . . . . . . :    CLE

Module information:
   Module creation date/time . . . . . . . . . . . . . :   94/01/13  13:50:14
   Source file . . . . . . . . . . . . . . . . . . . . :   C
      Library . . . . . . . . . . . . . . . . . . . . . :      MAYA
   Source member . . . . . . . . . . . . . . . . . . . :   TRY
   Source file change date/time . . . . . . . . . . . :   94/01/13  13:40:33
   Owner . . . . . . . . . . . . . . . . . . . . . . . :   MAYA
   Coded character set identifier . . . . . . . . . . . :   65535
   Text description . . . . . . . . . . . . . . . . . . :

   Machine instruction template included . . . . . . . :   *YES
   Sort sequence table . . . . . . . . . . . . . . . . :   *HEX
   Language identifier . . . . . . . . . . . . . . . . :   *JOBRUN
   Optimization level . . . . . . . . . . . . . . . . . :   *NONE
   Maximum optimization level . . . . . . . . . . . . . :   *FULL
   Debug data . . . . . . . . . . . . . . . . . . . . . :   *NO
   Compressed . . . . . . . . . . . . . . . . . . . . . :   *NO
   Program entry procedure name . . . . . . . . . . . . :   C_pep
   Number of parameters . . . . . . . . . . . . . . . . :   0       255
   Module state . . . . . . . . . . . . . . . . . . . . :   *USER
   Module domain . . . . . . . . . . . . . . . . . . . :   *SYSTEM
   Number of exported defined symbols . . . . . . . . . :   1
   Number of imported (unresolved) symbols . . . . . . :   15
Module compatibility:
   Module created on . . . . . . . . . . . . . . . . . :   V3R1M0
   Module created for . . . . . . . . . . . . . . . . . :   V2R3M0
   Earliest release module can be restored to . . . . . :   V2R3M0
```

Figure 11 - 5: Display module command

Q Can I have a module object with the same name as a program object?

A Yes, a module object can have the same name as a program or ILE service program because they are of different object types. The module object is of type *MODULE, whereas a program object is of type *PGM.

Q Will modules show up in the invocation stack?

A Yes, the Call Stack display will show the procedure, module, and bound program for ILE invocations. Activation groups are also displayed for all entries on the call stack. The display has been enhanced to provide alternative views for the additional information.

Q Why would you use CRTBNDxxx instead of CRTxxxMOD and CRTPGM?

A Use CRTBNDxxx when you are creating an ILE program that contains only one module. CRTBNDxxx is a one-step compile-and-bind creation similar to OPM's one-step compile process, except that you are invoking an ILE command with the CRTBNDxxx instead of an OPM command with CRTxxxPGM. CRTBNDxxx does create a *MODULE object, but the compiler discards it after the program is created. Use CRTxxxMOD and then CRTPGM when your program includes more than one module.

Q   Will removing observability prevent me from debugging my program?

A   If you completely remove a program's observability, you may not execute that program in debug mode. The same is true of programs created without debug information. If you want to delete just the portion of the object that may be necessary to re-create (or to change) the optimization levels and leave the information you need to be able to debug the object, use the CHGMOD, CHGPGM, or CHGSRVPGM command. Figure 11-6 shows the parameters of CHGMOD and CHGSRVPGM, and Figure 11-7 shows CHGPGM.

```
                        Change Module (CHGMOD)

Type choices, press Enter.

Module . . . . . . . . . . . .   AP            Name, generic*, *ALL
  Library  . . . . . . . . . .     DHAVITA     Name, *USRLIBL, *LIBL
Optimize module  . . . . . . .   *SAME         *SAME, *FULL, *BASIC, *NONE
Remove observable info . . . .   *SAME         *SAME, *ALL, *NONE...
Force module recreation  . . .   *NO           *NO, *YES
Text 'description' . . . . . .   *SAME

                      Change Service Program (CHGSRVPGM)

Type choices, press Enter.

Service program  . . . . . . .   G_L_P         Name, generic*, *ALL
  Library  . . . . . . . . . .     ANGELICA    Name, *USRLIBL
Optimize service program . . .   *NONE         *SAME, *FULL, *BASIC, *NONE
User profile . . . . . . . . .   *USER         *SAME, *USER, *OWNER
Use adopted authority  . . . .   *YES          *SAME, *YES, *NO
Remove observable info . . . .   *NONE         *SAME, *ALL, *CRTDTA...
Force recreation . . . . . . .   *NO           *NO, *YES
Text 'description' . . . . . .   'General Ledger Post for ANGELICA SYSTEMS'
```

Figure 11 - 6: Change module command to remove observability

As Figure 11-7 shows, with the CHGPGM command, you can delete *ALL observability information from the program object. In this case, the program will no longer be executable in debug mode.

```
                         Change Program (CHGPGM)
Type choices, press Enter.

Program  . . . . . . . . . . . .   AR            Name, generic*, *ALL
  Library  . . . . . . . . . .     MAYA          Name, *USRLIBL
Optimize program . . . . . . . .   *NONE         *SAME, *YES, *FULL, *BASIC...
User profile . . . . . . . . . .   *USER         *SAME, *USER, *OWNER
Use adopted authority  . . . . .   *YES          *SAME, *YES, *NO
Remove observable info . . . . .   *NONE         *SAME, *ALL, *CRTDTA...
Force program recreation . . . .   *NO           *NO, *YES
Text 'description' . . . . . . .   'Accounts Receivable for MAYA SYSTEMS'
```

Figure 11 - 7: Change program command to remove observability

Q   Will I be able to use the debugger on a non-interactive program?

A   Existing support for debugging such programs remains in the ILE debugger. The ILE debugger will support the STRSRVJOB (Start Service Job) command.

Exception Handling

Q   What is the intent of the ILE exception-handling model?

A   The ILE exception handling model lets you handle program exceptions in all ILE languages in a consistent manner. As we explained in Chapter 9, exceptions in ILE are translated into exception messages. You can take the following actions against those messages. Examine an exception message that the system has issued as a result of runtime error. Then you can

■ optionally modify the message to show that it has been received, or

- optionally recover from the exception by passing the exception message to a piece of code to take any necessary actions.

Q   What is an ILE condition?

A   Conditions provide cross-system consistency for high-level languages. You can, if you so wish, write ILE condition handlers to react to runtime error situations, ILE conditions will, of course, map to exception messages. ILE conditions are an SAA feature and are consistently represented by 12-byte data structures on any SAA participating system.

Q   Why would I want to provide my own condition handler?

A   By coding a condition handler, you can make your application more responsive to error situations. The example we gave in Chapter 10 was an application program that assumes a data file resides in a particular library on the system. If the program cannot find that file for file open, you receive a message giving you the opportunity to specify a new data file location. In this way, the message is more graceful than letting the system handle the condition, and often, the error is recoverable.

Q   What is the ILE RPG/400 exception-handling support?

A   The ILE RPG/400 compiler provides two types of exception-handling mechanisms: the error indicator handler and an error subroutine. These handlers address two types of exceptions: program exception and file exception. Some examples of program exceptions are division by zero, invalid array index, or square root of a negative number. Examples of file exceptions are undefined record type or a device error.

Miscellaneous

Q   Will I be able to execute my ILE programs on a previous release of OS/400?

A   No, ILE programs and service programs are valid only on V2R3 and later releases. The ability to create programs that execute on a previous release of OS/400 will remain as it is today for the non-ILE compilers. The ILE compilers will not create programs that can execute on a release of OS/400 previous to V2R3 because the required ILE runtime support does not exist there.

Q   Can I call OPM programs from my new ILE programs?

A   Yes, you can call existing OPM programs from ILE programs and ILE service programs. For example, in RPG, you use the CALL operation code. However, bear in mind that the call is dynamic, and the call performance from an ILE program to an OPM program will be comparable to calling an OPM program from another OPM program. Note also that an OPM program can call another OPM program, and a service program can call an OPM program.

Q   Will binding use more storage?

A   In general, the amount of DASD that production products use
should be comparable to the amount current programs use.
The actual amount of storage the executable part of a program
will require should be less than that used for current programs.
This will depend on how many modules are bound together,
how much function is contained within service programs, and
the level of optimization you used.

ILE programs on development machines, however, will require
more DASD because you will store modules as well as programs on those machines. Also, program objects will contain
more debugging information than with OPM programs.

Q   At create-module time, can I indicate a particular module as
the program entry procedure module?

A   Not explicitly. The CRTxxxMOD commands include no such parameter. However, you can indicate the program entry procedure module implicitly, as shown by the following example.
You issue the following CRTPGM command.

```
                          Create Program (CRTPGM)
Type choices, press Enter.

Program . . . . . . . . . . . .  NEW_CUST      Name
  Library . . . . . . . . . . .    TOPIWALA    Name, *CURLIB
  Module . . . . . . . . . . . .  GET_INFO      Name, generic*, *PGM, *ALL
  Library . . . . . . . . . . .    TOPIWALA    Name, *LIBL, *CURLIB...
                                 ASSIGN_NUM
                                   TOPIWALA
                                 VERIFY_UNQ
                                   TOPIWALA
            + for more values  ADD_NEW
                                   TOPIWALA
Text 'description' . . . . . . .  *ENTMODTXT

                          Additional Parameters

Program entry procedure module   *ONLY         Name, *ONLY, *FIRST
  Library . . . . . . . . . . .                 Name, *LIBL, *CURLIB...

Bind service program . . . . . .  *NONE         Name, generic*, *NONE, *ALL
  Library . . . . . . . . . . .                 Name, *LIBL
                  + for more values

Binding directory . . . . . . .  *NONE         Name, *NONE
  Library . . . . . . . . . . .                 Name, *LIBL, *CURLIB...
                  + for more values

Activation group . . . . . . . .  *NEW          Name, *NEW, *CALLER
Creation options . . . . . . . .                *GEN, *NOGEN, *NODUPPROC...
                  + for more values

Listing detail . . . . . . . . .  *NONE         *NONE, *BASIC, *EXTENDED...
Allow Update . . . . . . . . . .  *YES          *YES, *NO
User profile . . . . . . . . . .  *USER         *USER, *OWNER
Replace program . . . . . . . .  *YES          *YES, *NO
Authority . . . . . . . . . . .  *LIBCRTAUT     Name, *LIBCRTAUT, *CHANGE...
```

Figure 11 - 8: Create program command indicating PEP

As the above module list shows, the modules in Figure 11-9 are being bound together.

The program entry procedure module parameter on the CRTPGM panel shows a value of *ONLY. This value implies that only one of the modules listed contains a PEP. Furthermore, the *ONLY value is valid, providing that no more than one of the modules listed is an RPG module. In our

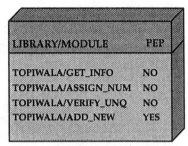

LIBRARY/MODULE	PEP
TOPIWALA/GET_INFO	NO
TOPIWALA/ASSIGN_NUM	NO
TOPIWALA/VERIFY_UNQ	NO
TOPIWALA/ADD_NEW	YES

Figure 11 - 9: Modules being bound

example, TOPIWALA/ADD_NEW is the module containing the PEP. ADD_NEW could be a C module or an RPG module. However, if ADD_NEW is an RPG module, then it can be the only RPG module being bound into the NEW_CUST program because a value of *ONLY is specified on the PEP parameter. If we specified more than one RPG module, the binder would return an error.

Now, let us follow this statement with an explanation: C programmers should be familiar with the concepts in the preceding paragraph. PC systems have supported the concept of binding for years. Are PEP parameters required on PC systems? How else can the programmer determine which module (or in PC terms, "OBJ") will gain execution control when the program is called? The answer is simple. Unlike RPG programs, C programs can contain multiple functions, each with it own local storage. The function main, however, is the function that gains control when a C program is called. If the programmer is binding together more than one C module (OBJ) to create a program, then only one should contain a main function. In this way, the system knows which function should gain execution control.

LIBRARY/MODULE	TYPE	Contains 'main'
TOPIWALA/GET_INFO	C	NO
TOPIWALA/ASSIGN_NUM	C	NO
TOPIWALA/VERIFY_UNQ	C	NO
TOPIWALA/ADD_NEW	C	YES

Figure 11 - 10: Valid combination with *ONLY specified on the program entry procedure parameter of CRTPGM

LIBRARY/MODULE	TYPE	Contains 'main'
TOPIWALA/GET_INFO	RPG	NO
TOPIWALA/ASSIGN_NUM	RPG	NO
TOPIWALA/VERIFY_UNQ	C	NO
TOPIWALA/ADD_NEW	C	YES

Figure 11 - 11: Invalid combination with *ONLY specified on the program entry procedure parameter of CRTPGM

Back to our example, the combination in Figure 11-10 would be a valid bind. The combinations in Figure 11-11, however, are invalid for the CRTPGM command when you specify a value of *ONLY on the program entry procedure parameter.

If we specified the *ONLY value on the program entry procedure parameter and all four modules were C modules, then only one should contain a main. Let's extend the rule we stated earlier to also state that if we are binding together more than one C module and *ONLY is specified on the program entry procedure parameter, then only one of those C modules should contain a main function. Also, if we are binding together one or more C modules with one or more RPG modules, we cannot specify *ONLY on the program entry procedure parameter of CRTPGM because the binder will return an error. The reason is that whenever we create an RPG module, we automatically create it with a program entry procedure. As a result, we can bind every RPG module, and call it from the command line because RPG has no equivalent to the C main function. It is for this reason that CRTPGM's default value for the program entry procedure parameter is *FIRST and not *ONLY. (*FIRST indicates that the first module the binder finds is the winner.) If all the modules were RPG modules, the first one specified must be the one intended to receive control. But in a mixed-language environment, you could specify several C modules (that didn't have a `main` and then an RPG module, and the binder would select the RPG module as the winner for the PEP on a *FIRST. If *ONLY were the default, we would receive an error whenever we attempted to bind together more than one RPG module using the *ONLY parameter value.

As a final note, when we use the *ONLY parameter on the CRTPGM command, the position of the module containing a program entry procedure in the module list is irrelevant.

ILE: A First Look

What's Next...

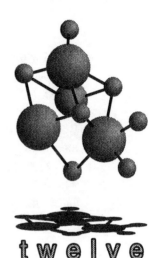

twelve

This introduction to ILE may make you wonder about the AS/400's future, so we'd like to give you our opinions. Let us first state that in no way should you assume that our ideas state IBM's plan. Rather, this is our speculation based on our understanding of ongoing development, industry demands, and IBM announcements.

We believe it would be a great error to think that the AS/400 and its key development languages were heading towards a maintenance-only mode. Given the enhancements to the environment, performance improvements, and movement towards a true application-delivery mindset, we think IBM is preparing for increased growth on this machine.

In the industry, interest in client-server computing is increasing rapidly. Discussions between IBM and AS/400 users have shown that users are enthusiastic about the AS/400's potential in a client-server configuration. As a result, IBM is considering the AS/400's involvement in this exciting new area.

Because the AS/400 is a very strong and proven database machine, AS/400 technology should be complementary to client-server computing. However, the AS/400 will continue to develop on its own, as well. Some areas of development lend themselves both to improving the AS/400 and to making it more suitable for a client-server environment.

For example, one weakness of the AS/400 in connection with client-server computing has been its interface. By requiring easy-to-program, easy-to-use graphical user interfaces, client-server computing will add value to the AS/400 in this area. Graphical front-end interfaces to the AS/400 seem to be the direction of the future as they can add convenience to your applications that take advantage of the AS/400's database and executing power.

Because of this emphasis on client-server computing and graphical user interfaces, we think AS/400 language development will explore the potential of graphical environments. ILE seems to be the first step in this direction, as it lays the groundwork for object-oriented programming (OOP) and visual programming. For instance, as we mentioned in Chapter 11, IBM is looking into the concept of a visual RPG environment.

The future of the key AS/400 development languages seems to lie in ease of development, ease of use, increasing functionality, and diversity. On today's AS/400, you can choose the OPM/EPM environment or ILE. In the future, you may also have other alternatives so that you can select the right language as well as the right environment for any task.

Appendix A: CL Commands

ILE-Related CL Commands	
Object/Command	**Command**
Modules	
Create	CRTxxxMOD
C Module	CRTCMOD
COBOL Module	CRTCBLMOD
RPG Module	CRTRPGMOD
Change Module	CHGMOD
Work with Module	WRKMOD
Display Module	DSPMOD
Delete Module	DLTMOD
Service Programs	
Create Service Program	CRTSRVPGM
Change Service Program	CHGSRVPGM
Work with Service Program	WRKSRVPGM
Display Service Program	DSPSRVPGM
Delete Service Program	DLTSRVPGM
Binding Directories	
Create Binding Directory	CRTBNDDIR
Add Binding Directory Entry	ADDBNDDIRE
Display Binding Directory	DSPBNDDIR
Work with Binding Directory	WRKBNDDIR
Work with Binding Directory Entry	WRKBNDDIRE
Remove Binding Directory Entry	RMVBNDDIRE
Delete Binding Directory	DLTBNDDIR

ILE-Related CL Commands	
Programs	
Create Program	CRTPGM
Create Bound Program	CRTBNDxxx
Create Bound C Program	CRTBNDC
Create Bound RPG Program	CRTBNDRPG
Create Bound COBOL Program	CRTBNDCBL
Change Program	CHGPGM
Work with Program	WRKPGM
Display Program	DSPPGM
Display Program References	DSPPGMREF
Delete Program	DLTPGM
Source Debugger	
Start Debug	STRDBG
Display Module Source	DSPMODSRC
End Debug	ENDDBG
SQL	
Create SQL ILE C Object	CRTSQLCI
Binder Language	
Start Programming Development Manager	STRPDM
Start Source Entry Utilit	STRSEU
Nonrunnable Binder Language Source File Commands	
Start Program Export	STRPGMEXP
Export	EXPORT
End Program Export	ENDPGMEXP

Appendix B: APIs

Activation-Group and Control-Flow APIs

CEE4ABN	Abnormal End
CEE4FCB	Find a Control Boundary
CEE4FCB	Register Activation Group Exit Procedure
CEERTX	Register Call Stack Entry Termination User Exit Procedure
CEETREC	Signal the Termination-Imminent Condition
CEEUTX	Unregister Call Stack Entry Termination User Exit Procedure

Condition-Management APIs

CEENCOD	Construct a Condition Token
CEEDCOD	Decompose a Condition Token
CEE4HC	Handle a Condition
CEEMRCR	Move the Resume Cursor to a Return Point
CEEHDLR	Register a User-Written Condition Handler
CEEGPID	Retrieve ILE Version and Platform ID
CEE4RIN	Return the Relative Invocation Number
CEESGL	Signal a Condition
CEEHDLU	Unregister a User Condition Handler

Date and Time APIs

CEEDYWK	Calculate Day-of-Week from Julian Date
CEEDAYS	Convert Date from Julian Date
CEEISEC	Convert Integers to Seconds
CEEDATE	Convert Julian Date to Character Format
CEEDATM	Convert Seconds to Character Timestamp
CEESECI	Convert Seconds to Integers
CEESECS	Convert Timestamp to Number of Seconds
CEEGMT	Get Current Greenwich Mean Time
CEELOCT	Get Current Local Time
CEEUTCO	Get Offset from Universal Time Coordinated to Local Time
CEEUTC	Get Universal Time Coordinated
CEEQCEN	Query Century
CEEFMDT	Return Default Date and Time Strings for Country
CEEFMDA	Return Default Date String for Country
CEEFMTM	Return Default Time String for Country
CEESCEN	Set Century

Math APIs

The x in the name of each math API refers to one of the following data types:

I 32-bit binary integer

S 32-bit single floating-point number

D 64-bit double floating-point number

T 32-bit single floating-complex number (both real and imaginary parts are 32 bits long)

E 64-bit double floating-complex number (both real and imaginary parts are 64 bits long)

Math APIs	
CEESxABS	Absolute Function
CEESxACS	Arccosine
CEESxASN	Arcsine
CEESxATN	Arctangent
CEESxAT2	Arctangent2
CEESxCGG	Conjugate of Complex
CEESxCOS	Cosine
CEESxCTN	Cotangent
CEESxERx	Error Function and its Complement
CEESxEXP	Exponential Base
CEESxXPx	Exponentiation
CEE4SIFAC	Factorial
CEESxDVD	Floating Complex Divide
CEESxMLT	Floating Complex Multiply
CEESxGMA	Gamma Function
CEESxATH	Hyperbolic Arctangent
CEESxCSH	Hyperbolic Cosine
CEESxSNH	Hyperbolic Sine
CEESxTNH	Hyperbolic Tangent
CEESxIMG	Imaginary Part of Complex
CEESxLGM	Log Gamma Function
CEESxLG1	Logarithm Base 10
CEESxLG2	Logarithm Base 2
CEESxLOG	Logarthm Base e
CEESxMOD	Modular Arithmetic
CEESxNIN	Nearest Integer
CEESxNWN	Nearest Whole Number
CEESxDIM	Positive Difference
CEESxSIN	Sine
CEESxSQT	Square Root
CEESxTAN	Tangent
CEESxSGN	Transfer of Sign
CEESxINT	Truncation
CEERAN0	Basic Random Number Generation (bindable)

Message-Handling APIs

CEEMOUT	Dispatch a Message
CEEMGET	Get a Message
CEEMSG	Get, Format, and Dispatch a Message

Program- or Procedure-Call APIs

CEEGSI	Get String Information
CEEDOD	Retrieve Operational Descriptor Information
CEETSTA	Test for Omitted Argument

Source-Debugger APIs

QteSubmitDebugCommand	Allow a Program to Issue Debug Statements
QteStartSourceDebug	Enables a Session to Use the Source Debugger
QteMapViewPosition	Map Positions from One View to Another
QteRegisterDebugView	Register a View of a Module
QteRemoveDebugView	Remove a View of a Module
QteRetrieveDebugAttribute	Retrieve the Attributes of the Source Debug Session
QteRetrieveModuleViews	Retrieve the List of Modules and Views for a Program
QteRetrieveStoppedPosition	Retrieve the Position Where the Program Stopped
QteRetrieveViewText	Retrieve Source Text from the Specified View
QteSetDebugAttribute	Set the Attributes of the Source Debug Session
QteEndSourceDebug	Take a Job out of Debug Mode

Storage-Management APIs

CEECRHP	Create Heap
CEE4DAS	Define Heap Allocation Strategy
CEEDSHP	Discard Heap
CEEFRST	Free Storage
CEEGTST	Get Heap Storage
CEEMKHP	Mark Heap
CEECZST	Reallocate Storage
CEERLHP	Release Heap

Glossary

Activation Group The environment within which ILE programs are executed. The system creates an ILE activation group before the execution of an application and awards the activation group all the necessary resources to execute that program, including dynamic, static, and automatic storage. You can think of the activation group as a substructure that comes into existence only for the purpose of program execution.

Activation-Group-Level Scoping Determines what components of an activation group are visible outside the activation group. Occurs when a resource is actually connected, or allocated, to the activation group of an ILE program or service program.

Automatic Storage An area of storage the system allocates for a program or procedure that has been called to execute. Unlike static storage, automatic storage is redefined each time the program or procedure is called.

Automatic Variables Variables residing in automatic storage. They exist only during the execution of the procedure or program in which they are declared.

Binder A system facility that ties together multiple modules to form one program. The CRTPGM (Create Program) and CRTSRVPGM (Create Service Program) commands activate the binder as part of the compile process.

Binder Language A language consisting of a set of commands that let you specify the procedures and data items that this program can export (i.e., defines the external or public interface for an ILE program). To define the public interface, the binder language explicitly indicates which variables and procedure or function names will be externalized (specified as exports) to the user (program) of the program. Binder source, written in ILE binder language, is used as input to CRTSRVPGM and CRTPGM. The binder source you create in the binder language cannot be executed.

Binding
The activity of taking the modules that are to be bound by copy and the names of any service programs that are needed at bind time and creating a bound program or service program from the copied module objects. CRTPGM/CRTSRVPGM initiates binding.

Binding Directory
A list of names of service programs and modules that the system will use to resolve import and export references during the creation of other ILE programs. The binding directory is a battery of tried-and-proven modules and service programs that the developer will reuse often in developing applications.

Bound Program
An executable program (object type, *PGM) created with the CRTPGM command and consisting of one module (object type, *MODULE) or more.

Breakpoint
A debugger term. As the program is executing under debug mode in OS/400, you can specify a point (the breakpoint) where the program will pause from execution, thereby allowing you to control further execution. Some activities you might perform at a breakpoint might be to examine the contents of program variables, the call stack, and registers. Breakpoints are removable so that you may continue without pausing execution at the same point.

Call
Adds a new entry on the ILE call stack and passes execution control to the procedure or program that has been called.

Call Stack
A snapshot of a job that is executing programs or procedures. The call stack is a last-in, first-out structure and represents the call order of the programs or procedures executing at some moment in time. One program or procedure executing in a job is referred to as a *call stack entry*.

Call Stack Entry
A program or procedure executing within a given job on the system. Call stack entries map to procedures or programs as they were called within the current job. The call stack gives the call order. Call stack entries provide information, such as local and automatic variables and active condition handlers.

Condition
A system-independent representation of an error as it exists in a high-level language. In ILE, conditions map to exception messages.

Condition Handler
A user-written routine that is useful in the implementation of user-written procedures that the system will activate or that will respond upon receiving an ILE condition for a particular call stack entry. You can register condition handlers, or put them into effect, during runtime. See also *condition*.

Condition Token
In ILE, a data structure that maps to an ILE exception message and contains relevant information about the error, and this information is derived from the exception message itself. You can think of conditions and condition tokens as a layer over the ILE exception message ar-

chitecture for creating and maintaining application consistency across all SAA systems.

Control Boundary

In terms of ILE activation groups, a control boundary is any call stack entry for which the nearest preceding call stack entry resides in a different activation group. In terms of the OPM default activation group, a control boundary is any call stack entry for which the nearest preceding call stack entry is an OPM program.

Debug

The process of searching for and removing errors in an executable program.

Debug Mode

Any environment in which the host system gives you information about the execution of a program you are debugging. Examples of such information would be contents of program variables, system registers, call stack. Essentially, executing a program in debug mode lets you pause the execution of that program so that you may perform debug actions, such as examining variable content and program instructions.

Direct Monitor Handler

A monitor for ILE program exceptions. In ILE, you use or activate direct monitor handlers for some given segment of an HLL program.

Dynamic Program Call

Passes execution control to a program other than the one making the call. That is, the calling program does not contain the entry point being called. In RPG/400, for example, when you use the CALL operation code, it will execute a different program (*PGM object) from the one that contains the CALL. In ILE, you can call procedures that are part of a module object with a CALLB (Call Bound) operation, but a dynamic call must be to an object of type *PGM.

Dynamic Screen Management	Control of screen interaction through the use of ILE APIs.
Entry Point	The point at which execution enters into a program. In other words, the first point in a program that is executed when that program is called. RPG programs have one entry point. C programs can have more than one entry point, providing the source module does not contain a main function.
EPM (Extended Program Model)	A development and execution environment built as a layer over OPM for the promotion of procedural calls in application programs.
Export	A symbol (i.e. procedure, function, variable) that is defined in one module (the exporting module) and can be used in (imported into) other modules that have been bound together with the exporting module to form a *PGM or *SRVPGM object. A symbol can be exported from a module object and from a service program. From a service program, you can export only a symbol from a *MODULE object that has been bound by copy into a *SRVPGM. So, only the set of symbols exported by a service program's bound-by-copy modules can be candidates to be exported from the service program.
Extended Program Model (EPM)	See EPM
External Message Queue	An ILE message queue that all programs and procedures executing within a job use for the purpose of receiving and sending messages that are not part of that job. Messages between an interactive job and the workstation are an example.

External Symbol
A name found in a program. This name represents, but is not limited to, a program, procedure, function, or variable outside this program. An external symbol is important during the bind step in ILE program creation because external references must be resolved. That is, an external symbol must be connected to other modules that are being bound together with the referencing module to form an ILE program or service program. In order to successfully create a program, the modules to which external references are connected must have imports specified to match the external symbols.

File
A storage structure that groups together source members and other objects in the system.

Handle Cursor
Points to the current exception handler during program execution.

Heap
Dynamic memory that the system allocates to a procedure for execution. Owned by activation groups, heaps are destroyed when the activation group is deleted. Usually, heap storage is in the form of a heap data structure. That is, it grows upwards and shrinks downwards.

Heap Identifier
An ILE-specific term. A number referring to a particular heap within an activation group.

Import
Reference to a variable, procedure, or function that is not defined in the referencing module. Imports are matched with exports during the symbol resolution phase of binding.

ILE (Integrated Language Environment)
The Integrated Language Environment is a set of constructs and interfaces that provides a common runtime and bindable APIs for all ILE languages.

Local Data   Data that may be used only by the procedure, function, module, or program in which the data is defined. If data is local to a given module, the module defining the local data does not share this data with other modules bound into the program that contains the defining module. By this definition, it is also said that local data is *scoped* to the module in which it is defined. The concept of localized data is not restricted to ILE.

Local Variable   A variable that is defined in the module, function, or procedure in which it is used. If a local variable is defined in a module, other modules may not reference that local data. The same holds true if the local variable is defined at a function or procedure level. That is, other functions or procedures within that module cannot reference that local variable.

Job   A unit of work on a computer system. Usually the system gives jobs system resource (such as storage and processor time) separately from other jobs that may be executing. In ILE, a job is necessary to execute any program. A job contains an *activation group* in ILE.

Module   On the AS/400, the nonexecutable object (of type *MODULE) that results from compiling an ILE source program by executing a CRTxxxMOD command. Modules are not executable until they are bound into an ILE program or ILE service program by means of the CRTPGM or CRTSRVPGM command. The resulting program is only then executable. On other systems, a module may be a program object that has one entry point, and any calls to other programs or subprograms are external calls.

Nested Exception   An exception that occurs during the handling of some other exception.

Observability For an object residing on a system, the information stored with the object that makes the source used to create that object retrievable. You can symbolically debug objects that carry observability information. You can remove observability information from an object.

Open Data Path (ODP) A control block the system creates upon opening a file. The ODP contains information such as merged file attributes and any codes or information returned from input or output operations. The ODP control block ceases to exist once the file is closed.

Operational Descriptor Usually, arguments passed to some function, procedure, or program. Operational descriptors carry information about an argument, such as its size, structure (layout), or type. Extremely useful when the receiving procedure, function, or program cannot deduce such information on its own but requires it to carry out its own designed tasks.

OPM (Original Programming Model) The development and runtime programming environment for a set of high-level languages called the OPM high-level languages. The AS/400 was introduced in 1988 with this environment. ILE, in some senses, complements or replaces OPM, on which many of the functions contained or introduced in ILE were founded.

Optimization Usually, activities that some high-level-language compiler carries out to make the generated executable code faster or more efficient. You could optimize this example program segment (part of optimization)

```
x = 3 ;
y = x + 9 ;
z = 6/x + y ;
a = y / 7 ; ...
```

in the following manner:

```
x = 3 ;
y = 12 ;
z = 14 ;
a = 2 ;
```

Such optimization is called constant folding and is just one type of optimization that a compiler may perform. Compiler optimization is possible only when all information is available at compile time, as in our example above.

Optimization Level

The measurable degree to which a compiler optimizes generated code. The optimization level can be important during the compilation phase because the time required for compiles can sometimes be greatly affected if large optimizations are requested.

Parameter, Passed by Reference

In ILE, *parameter* is the identifier that defines the type of arguments that are passed to a called procedure. Generally, the term refers to a value passed to any called procedure, function, or program, and this value then serves as input. Or, if *passed by reference*, the parameter serves as a pointer to a storage location whose content the called procedure, function, or program will change.

PEP

See Program Entry Procedure

Program Entry Procedure (PEP)

A procedure that a high-level language compiler generates and gives to some module. This procedure may, but does not have to, serve as the main entry point for the program that is being compiled and that incorporates that module.

Percolation

A process that occurs during exception and condition handling. If a program, procedure, or function currently executing on a system declines to handle an exception message or condition, that exception or condition is passed to the next lower entry in the call stack for handling. This process, *percolation*, continues until some condition handler associated with a call stack entry handles the exception or condition.

Procedure

A callable code segment within a program, a *procedure* is designed to carry out some task and then return to the caller. The compiler for which the procedure was written may also support parameters and return values. A procedure is contained within a *MODULE object. Since modules are not executable, the module must be bound into a *PGM or *SRVPGM object before the procedure can be called.

Procedure Call

A call to a procedure and, in ILE, to a procedure contained within a module or bound program.

Procedure Pointer Call

A function (that some HLL compilers support) that lets you specify the address of some procedure to be called. Because the procedure pointer is applied dynamically, you can manipulate tables of procedure addresses such that you can decide at runtime which procedure will be called. See also *procedure call* and *procedure call, static*.

Procedure Call, Static

A high-level language call to some procedure bound into the program in which the call occurs. The procedure name being called is resolved to some actual storage address during bind time.

Program   In ILE, an executable object of type *PGM that was created from the binding together of separately compiled HLL modules by means of the CRTPGM command.

Program Call   In ILE, a call to an ILE or OPM program, i.e., to an object of type *PGM.

Program Call,   A call from one program to another program. The name
Dynamic   of the program is resolved to an actual storage location during execution time, as opposed to bind time.

Public Interface   The names of the exported procedures and data items that can be accessed by ILE objects.

Resolved Import   An import whose type and name exactly match the type and name of an export.

Resume Cursor   A system pointer that marks the programmed instruction point at which execution will resume after the handling of an exception.

Resume Point   The point at which execution will resume after the handling of an exception.

Return   During execution, causes the system to remove the call stack entry associated with the program, procedure, or function containing the return and pass execution control back to the previous call stack entry.

Roll Back   If an application program or user has changed data, a roll back restores that data to the state at its last commitment boundary.

SAA   See Systems Application Architecture.

Scope   The delimited extent to which the semantic effects of programmed instructions can reach. Scope can refer to procedures, functions, programs, activation groups, and jobs.

Service Program A bound ILE program of object type *SRVPGM that performs utility-type functions that provide procedures and data items that other bound programs or service programs can reference. Service programs' benefits include well-defined interfaces, maintainability, and the ability to hide internal complexity from using programs.

Signature   A number generated by the system, a signature identifies a service program's supported interfaces (i.e., what objects a service program can interact with), based on the sequential ordering of that service program's exports. Signatures make level checking possible for service programs; that is, signatures provide a means for the users of service programs to determine whether they should recreate their application programs that use a service program when its public interface has changed.

Source Debugger A program-development tool that lets you see the content of variables and currently executing instructions, as well as the actual HLL source code, during program execution, so that you can spot and correct problems.

Source Member   The object in which AS/400 program source code resides.

Stack   A structure that accepts data on a last-in, first-out (LIFO) basis. That is, the last item is the first retrievable item from that data structure.

Static Storage   An area of storage the system creates when a particular program, function, or procedure is called for the first time. Each program, procedure, or function can have its own static and automatic storage. Static storage, unlike automatic storage, is defined only once per activation and is residual after the called program, procedure, or function returns. That is, the system retains the content of storage locations within static storage.

Static Variables Variables that are declared for a program activation. Also, in ILE, each activation group can maintain its own static variables for programs within the containing job.

Strong Export A strong export is an export for which only one definition of the required symbol is permitted during bindtime. The first definition is chosen; other, duplicate, definitions are ignored.

Symbol Resolution The process of matching the set of imported symbol names of the modules to be bound by copy with the set of exported symbol names from the specified modules, service programs, or modules of service programs, that are specified in binding directories.

Systems Application Architecture (SAA) An architecture defining a set of rules guiding the design of a common user interface, programming interface, application programs, and communications support for IBM strategic operating systems, such as OS/2 and OS/400.

Translation An OS/400 term that describes the final step in the compilation process. Converts a program's HLL source instructions to an executable form. ILE terminology refers to the translator as the *optimizing translator.*

UEP See user entry procedure.

User Entry Procedure (UEP) A programmer-written entry procedure (in C, the main procedure) that is the specific target of a dynamic program call. It is the UEP that gains execution control from the PEP (Program Entry Procedure). See also *Program Entry Procedure*, for contrast.

Index

D

R

S

Notes

Notes

Notes

Notes

Notes

Notes

Notes

Notes

Notes

Notes